LIBRARY
University of Glasgow

ALL ITEMS ARE ISSUED SUBJECT TO RECALL

GUL 18-08

Language, Names, and Information

The Blackwell/Brown Lectures in Philosophy

The Blackwell/Brown Lectures in Philosophy present compact books distilling cutting-edge research from across the discipline. Based on public lectures presented at Brown University, the books in the series are by established scholars of the highest caliber, presenting their work in a clear and concise format.

1. *Semantic Relationism* by Kit Fine
2. *The Philosophy of Philosophy* by Timothy Williamson
3. *Language, Names, and Information* by Frank Jackson

Forthcoming books by Philip Pettit, and John Broome

Language, Names, and Information

Frank Jackson

WILEY-BLACKWELL

A John Wiley & Sons, Ltd., Publication

This edition first published 2010
© 2010 Frank Jackson

Blackwell Publishing was acquired by John Wiley & Sons in February 2007. Blackwell's publishing program has been merged with Wiley's global Scientific, Technical, and Medical business to form Wiley-Blackwell.

Registered Office
John Wiley & Sons Ltd, The Atrium, Southern Gate, Chichester, West Sussex, PO19 8SQ, United Kingdom

Editorial Offices
350 Main Street, Malden, MA 02148-5020, USA
9600 Garsington Road, Oxford, OX4 2DQ, UK
The Atrium, Southern Gate, Chichester, West Sussex, PO19 8SQ, UK

For details of our global editorial offices, for customer services, and for information about how to apply for permission to reuse the copyright material in this book please see our website at www.wiley.com/wiley-blackwell.

The right of Frank Jackson to be identified as the author of this work has been asserted in accordance with the UK Copyright, Designs and Patents Act 1988.

Library of Congress Cataloging-in-Publication Data

Jackson, Frank, 1943–
    Language, names, and information / Frank Jackson.
        p. cm. – (The Blackwell/Brown lectures in philosophy ; 3)
    Includes bibliographical references and index.
    ISBN 978-1-4051-6158-9 (hardcover : alk. paper)   1. Discourse analysis.
2. Psycholinguistics.   3. Consciousness.   4. Linguistics–Methodology.   I. Title.
    P302.J323 2010
    121'.68—dc22
                                    2010006822

A catalogue record for this book is available from the British Library.

Set in 10.5/13 pt Sabon by Toppan Best-set Premedia Limited
Printed and bound in Malaysia by Vivar Printing Sdn Bhd

01   2010

For Charlotte and Stella

Contents

Prologue

When I read Saul Kripke's *Naming and Necessity* and Hilary Putnam's "The Meaning of 'Meaning'", they seemed to me, as they did to so many, to be enormously insightful contributions to the philosophy of language.[1] However, although I had much company in coming to this judgment, I found that I was in the minority when it came to articulating the important lessons we should take away from these publications. I saw (after a good deal of reflection) Kripke as teaching us that proper names are typically sources of information about what they name, a message that fits nicely with the description theory of reference for proper names, *provided* that the descriptions in question are spelt out in terms of causal connections that carry information. The majority saw Kripke as refuting any version of the description theory. The one thing we did seem to be in agreement about was that Kripke had taught us that proper names are rigid designators.

I saw Putnam as teaching us that the reference of names of kinds often goes by underlying nature, especially scientifically significant underlying nature, not by the properties that first led us to postulate the kinds in question. The message was that it is a mistake to hold, for example, that "acid" refers to any substance that has the properties that led chemists to introduce the term into chemical theory. "Acid" refers, rather, to the kind that typically explains those properties, or properties like those properties.[2] This does not mean that the reference of "acid" doesn't go by known properties. We know that there is a kind underlying and explaining the properties that led chemists to introduce the category *acid*. Being such a kind is,

---

[1] Kripke (1980); Putnam (1975).
[2] The properties need not be quite as we first thought of course.

therefore, a known property. It means, rather, that some substance counts as an acid if it is of the kind, or a kind, that typically underlies the manifest properties, even if it does not itself have the manifest properties.[3] Equally, something can have all the properties that led to the introduction of the category but fail to be an acid by virtue of not being of the kind that typically underlies the properties. Moreover, although this is an important fact about the reference of many terms in science, it isn't an essential feature. The concept of a *vitamin* is a significant one in the science of nutrition but it is not true that "vitamin" refers to a unified explanatory kind or kinds. However, the lesson the majority seemed to take away was that the reference doesn't go by known properties at all. But my biggest disagreement with the majority was over the significance of the Twin Earth thought experiment that Putnam used to cement his 'reference goes by kinds' message. The majority, and Putnam himself, took the thought experiment to provide a compelling argument for externalism about linguistic content, and, in subsequent developments, for externalism about mental content. I dissented, and in addition was puzzled by the insouciance with which many were prepared to abandon narrow content. As we will see later (in Lecture Five), we need narrow content.

Over the years I have defended my dissenting opinions,[4] and, while being in the minority, I have been far from alone in my dissent. Indeed, sometimes in expressing my dissent I have found myself saying, in my own words and from my own take on the issues, what others have said, in one way or another. The kind and much appreciated invitation to give the Blackwell/Brown Lectures in Philosophy gave me the opportunity to put things I have said in various places into a coherent package, and that is what I sought to do in the lectures. Moreover, since giving the lectures, as a result of reflection on the discussions arising at them and subsequent discussions with colleagues and friends, and at conferences and departmental seminars, and with my graduate students, I came to realize two things that were not clear (or not clear enough) to me when I gave the lectures.

One is that there are two quite different things you might mean by the description theory of reference for proper names. On one

---

[3] And not just for the uninteresting reason that it is highly diluted.
[4] Jackson (1980, 1994, 1998a, 1998b, 2003, 2005, 2007b)

reading, the theory is certainly false. On the other, it is, I will be arguing, true. I will say a little about these two readings near the end of the first lecture and in more detail in the final lecture (Lecture Five).

The other thing I came to realize was that, in the dissenting papers already mentioned, I had not sufficiently emphasized that in order to make good sense of the debate about proper names, over names of kinds, and the debate over narrow versus broad content, one needs to set the debate explicitly within an overall approach to meaning and reference, an overall approach to the question, What *precisely* is our subject when we discuss questions of meaning and reference? Consulting and swapping intuitions about what various sentences and words mean, in the absence of a view about what it is that we are debating when we discuss different views about meaning and reference, does not, I came to realize, get us very far.

The overall approach of these lectures might be called *the informational-cum-representational-framework*. I will say a good deal about this framework in the lectures to come, but the core idea is that a language is a system of representation that delivers putative information about how things are to those who understand the language. The most important thing about the sentence "There is a land mine one meter from your left foot" is how it represents things to be, the information it carries, in a way that is accessible to those competent in English. In philosophizing about meaning and reference, we need to keep this insight center stage, or so it seems to me. This implies, for example, that the crucial question for any account of proper names is whether or not it captures correctly how users of the name represent things to be, the putative information they deliver, when they use the name in declarative sentences.

I have just spoken of what I will do in the lectures to come rather than what I will do in the chapters that follow. This is partly to mark the origins of this book in a set of lectures, albeit a set of three rather than the set of five lectures that make up this volume, but mainly to signal that what is to come is very much in lecture format. I have deliberately kept the tone conversational and informal. Of course there are footnotes, but I have tried to minimize their number. Of course there are technicalities, but I have tried to corral them and to say things in ordinary English as much as possible. Although Kripke's and Putnam's seminal publications carry surprisingly little technical baggage, subsequent discussions have, understandably and properly, sometimes become quite technical. This means that I cannot avoid a certain amount of technical entanglement – we will, for example, need to talk on occasion of functions from worlds to truth values, and of functions from centered worlds to truth values, in discussing two-dimensionalism. However, my belief is that the key points can, in the main, be made in terms the folk – that's you and me when we aren't being professional philosophers, cognitive scientists, psychologists, or whatever – understand. This is as it should be. Our subject is natural language, the language of the folk, not quantum mechanics or the foundations of mathematics.

I have many debts. To my lecturers in *Introduction to Statistics*, and later to Robert Stalnaker and David Lewis in their publications, for teaching me about the possible worlds way of thinking of information and representation, and more generally of the world-directed nature of much of language.[5] To Martin Davies, Lloyd Humberstone, and Pavel Tichý for teaching me about two-dimensionalism.[6] To my graduate students, as already mentioned. To a reading group at ANU. To too many colleagues and friends to name, but I must list (in addition to those already mentioned): David Braddon-Mitchell, David Chalmers, Simon Cullen, Michael Devitt, Andy Egan, Fred Kroon, Philip Pettit, Brian Rabern, Denis Robinson, Michael Smith, Daniel Stoljar, and Wong Kai-yee. To the very helpful comments from two readers for Wiley-Blackwell. I am indebted to Scott Soames in a rather different way. His trenchant criticisms of the description theory of reference (2002, 2005a, 2005b) forced me to get clearer about what that theory was, and made me realize the need for these lectures. It goes without saying, but I will say it all the same, I alone am responsible.

Princeton, November 2009

---

[5]   See, e.g., Stalnaker (1984) and Lewis (1986).
[6]   Davies and Humberstone (1980 and in conversation), Tichý (1983).

Lecture One

The Debate Over the Theory of Reference for Proper Names

1. Where we will make our start

This lecture sets the scene for the lectures to come by drawing some morals from, and giving something of a running commentary on, the vigorous debate over the description theory of reference for proper names. It will explain why I dissent from the majority about the anti-description theory message allegedly delivered by Kripke. I don't think he refuted the description theory of reference for proper names. I think he, in effect, told us which version of the description theory we should affirm. Near the end, I will talk about the key distinction, heralded in the prologue, between two quite different things you might mean by the description theory of reference for proper names.

2. The supervenience of reference on nature

I start with something I feel should be relatively non-contentious, although, as we will see, it has contentious implications.

The debate over the description theory of reference for proper names is not about whether the reference of proper names goes by description (in the sense of going by properties, the availability of a *word* or *phrase* for the property that settles reference on a description theory isn't in itself to the point). We know that the reference of proper names goes by description. That follows from the supervenience of reference on nature. If a token name "N" refers to x but not to y, x and y must differ in some way, and in some way over and above the difference that the first but not the second is that to which "*N*" refers. There must be something about *x*, a feature of *x*, which explains why "*N*" refers to it and not to *y*.

The point here isn't one about verification. We aren't playing a Viennese waltz. True, if *per impossible* "*N*" referred to *x* and not *y*, in the case where *x* and *y* are exactly alike, one could never find out which of the two "*N*" named. But what is crucial is not the epistemological point but, rather, that there would be nothing to make the difference, and a difference in terms of what is referred to isn't arbitrary. Insisting that there might still be a fact of the matter as to which "*N*" named would be like insisting that exactly one of:

> Had Bizet and Verdi been compatriots, they would both have been French

and

> Had Bizet and Verdi been compatriots, they would both have been Italian

must be true. The mistake in insisting that exactly one of the above sentences must be true, no matter how symmetrical the situation may be, isn't to do with verification problems (though they would exist, of course); it is to do with arbitrariness.[1]

The difference in nature between *x* and *y* when "*N*" refers to one and not the other may be in their relational properties. Tweedledum and Tweedledee are, we may suppose, qualitative duplicates (not that they are in Lewis Carroll, *Through the Looking Glass*; they are same sayers and maybe mirror images). All the same, they have different names. "Tweedledum" will refer to one of them and not the other; ditto for "Tweedledee." The explanation will lie in the different relational properties they possess. To say exactly which differences are crucial would trespass on matters for later discussion. But among the differences are the following: Tweedledum but not Tweedledee was baptized "Tweedledum";[2] Tweedledum but not Tweedledee

---

[1] See Goodman (1947).

[2] I mean "baptize" in the sense of giving a name to, not in the sense of admission to the Christian Church. See Kripke (1980).

answers to the name "Tweedledum"; Tweedledum but not Tweedledee is the object that sentences containing "Tweedledum" carry information about; and so on. The fact that "Tweedledum" refers to Tweedledum and not to Tweedledee is not a counter-example to the supervenience of reference on nature but instead illustrates the fact that the nature in question has to be understood so as to include the relations between what is referred to and the token name in question (excluding of course the very relation of being what the name names – that would trivialize the supervenience of reference on nature). We might also have a case of qualitative identity with difference in reference where the name is one and the same. Paris Texas and Paris France are very different. But they might have been qualitative duplicates. Consistent with this, it might have been the case that some tokens of "Paris" refer to the first city, and other tokens of "Paris" to the second city. There will, in that case, be a difference in the relationship between the respective *tokens* and the respective cities. Causal theorists will tell us that the difference lies in which Paris is in a certain causal connection to which tokens. We will be saying something similar in due course, but from a perspective friendly to the description theory.

It follows from the supervenience of reference on nature that, whenever a name refers to an object, there is a property of that object such that the name refers to an object if and only if the object has the property (in the inclusive sense of a property that includes relational properties). In that sense, a description theory of reference for names has to be true.[3] What then is the debate about?

3. The availability issue

The debate is – can only be – about the *availability* of the property or description that settles the reference. Supervenience is compatible with unknowability. If names were assigned to objects by some secret process constrained only by a respect for supervenience – imagine that names are paired one–one with uniquely possessed properties by an evil demon who won't talk, and that each name refers to the object with the property the demon pairs the name with – then the

---

[3] The same goes, of course, for token indexicals and demonstratives.

reference-determining property for any given name would be unavail-
able (except to the demon, and he's not talking), but supervenience
would be respected. There would no difference in reference without
a difference in referent.

But the anti-description theorists' position isn't – had better not
be – that the relevant property is not available to anyone ever. Unless
we are to give up entirely on finding a theory of reference for proper
names, we are committed to the availability, to some person at some
time, of a truth of the form: "N" refers to x if and only if ... , where
the ellipsis is filled with a property specification or description that
says how x must be to be that to which "N" refers. That's what a
theory of reference for a proper name *is*. For example, those who say
something like, " 'N' refers to x if and only if x was baptized 'N' (or
with a name with so and so a relation to 'N') in the past, and speakers of the language have agreed to use later tokens of 'N' in such and
such a way" are giving one account of how to fill in the ellipsis; those
who say something like, " 'N' refers to x if and only if 'N' is associated with a property P that x alone has" are giving another account
of how to fill in the ellipsis. But the framework is the same in both
cases. To provide a theory of reference *is* to provide the property that
determines what a name refers to; it is, that is, to provide the conditions under which a name refers to what it does refer to.[4] This means
that to hold that we will never know the property that determines
the reference of a name is to hold that we will never know the correct
theory of reference for names. We might as well stop searching right
now.

It follows that the only plausible version of anti-descriptivism
affirms that the reference-determining property for a name is *relatively* inaccessible. The version allows that some know the property,
namely, those in possession of the correct theory of reference for
the name, but many, perhaps most, don't know the reference-
determining property. Thus many of those opponents of the description theory who favor some version of the causal theory respond,
when asked why their theory isn't a kind of description theory – the
kind known as causal descriptivism[5] – that the causal story is not
known by the folk. We know it, they say, but most do not, and give

[4]   *Cf.* Robert Nozick's point mentioned by Kripke (1980, p. 88, *n*.88.)
[5]   For causal descriptivism see, e.g., Kroon (1987; 2009).

as examples the names "Feynman" and "Jonah." They argue that certain tokens of "Feynman" in the mouths and from the pens of the folk refer to Feynman, the physicist, but the folk do not know any property unique to Feynman, and hence do not know the reference-determining property, for that property must be unique to Feynman.[6]

The trouble for this "we know but they don't" position is that the folk *do* know a property unique to Feynman. The folk know perfectly well that sentences like "Feynman worked at CalTech" carry information about Feynman. This is obvious from the use they make of these sentences. This knowledge is as commonplace as the knowledge that what appears on television screens carries information (or putative information, but I will often drop the "putative"; it gets tedious). What is more, they know that information transmission is underpinned by causal connections. Someone watching a tennis match on television does not need to be told that the information they are getting about the match depends on causal links between what is happening on court and what is happening on the screen. What is more, the folk know that the information about an object carried by sentences containing proper names typically depends on causal chains initiated by the assignment of a name to the object. They know that the information carried by names requires *naming*. What is more, they know the information carried relies on their language community adopting conventions of usage that mean that sentences containing names preserve information about what is named.

What makes it especially clear that the folk know all this is what they *do* when they hear a sentence like "Feynman worked at CalTech." They repeat it and, being good citizens, they would hardly repeat it unless they thought it carried information, and they would be slightly bemused if asked who or what it carried information about – "The person called 'Feynman' of course." If the folk happen to know that CalTech is in Pasadena, they may well go on to utter the sentence "Feynman worked in Pasadena." In doing this, they are participating in the conventions that underlie the transmission of information using names, and, when they do it, they don't need a tutorial from philosophers of language first.

This is very much in line with what Kripke says (see especially 1980, p. 91). Although he doesn't say it this way, Kripke's account

---

[6] See, e.g., Devitt (forthcoming); Devitt and Sterelny (1999); Soames (2005b, p. 299)

is one that makes proper names part of what Timothy Williamson calls "a channel for the acquisition of knowledge" (2007, p. 264).[7] And it is this picture that tells us why "Madagascar" refers to Madagascar and not the part of Africa originally named "Madagascar." Sentences of the form "So and so happened in Madagascar" carry information about Madagascar, not about the part of Africa. (I assume that Evans's (1973) account of the history of the use of "Madagascar" is correct; if it isn't, please pretend that it is.) Had there been a major earthquake in Madagascar last night, today's papers and internet sites would contain sentences like "Many died in Madagascar overnight" and "Relief pours into Madagascar." However, sentences like these would not have appeared had the major earthquake taken place in the relevant part of Africa. None of this is news to the folk – surely. Or suppose I hear the name "Napoleon" and decide it would be a nice name for my pet aardvark, I don't refer to Napoleon even if the token I heard was a use that referred to Napoleon.[8] The reason is that my uses of "Napoleon," stemming from the decision to use it for my pet aardvark, will carry information about the aardvark and not Napoleon.

A way to bring this out is to imagine that I am quite wrong. Imagine, that is, that a causal, information-preserving account of the reference of proper names that appeals to the role of naming, plus observing the convention of transmitting information using names, is correct but is not known by the folk. Information is valuable. People want it and pay for it. If names are key sources of information about objects but this is something known only to certain philoso-phers, we, or they, should be shouting the news from the roof tops, or, at the least, sending e-mails to colleagues in other departments passing on the good news. How could we reasonably restrict our-selves to talking about it in philosophy seminars? But of course no philosopher is going to send an e-mail to, say, the Politics Department in their university telling them that the appearance in the papers of sentences like "Gordon Brown increased funding for Barclays Bank yesterday" carries information about Gordon Brown, and does so in virtue of an information-preserving causal chain involving the names

---

[7]   See also Kroon (2009), Evans (1973; 1982, ch. 11); the basic idea can be found in many places, as you would expect if it is a bit of folk wisdom.
[8]   The example is a modification of one of Kripke's (1980, p. 96).

given to Brown and to Barclays, and the observing of conventions for the transmission of information. (Imagine the reaction of the Politics Department.)

Similar points apply to the famous "Jonah" example (Kripke 1980, p. 67f.). Many causal theorists distinguish themselves from causal descriptivists by insisting that, although the reference of certain tokens of "Jonah" go by a certain causal property related to a certain naming some time in the past, this property is only known to a few. In particular, it isn't known by the folk. However, as one would expect, there has been considerable interest over the years in whether Jonah, the Jonah of the *Bible*, existed, and if he did who he was. The same goes for Helen of Troy. Scholars pursuing these questions have never felt the need to employ philosophers of language to help them in their search for the Jonah of the *Bible* or for Helen of Troy. But the task of finding who, if anyone, Jonah or Helen were is nothing other than the task of finding who, if anyone, fits the bill to be the referent of "Jonah" or "Helen" in certain texts, and fitting the bill is having the right properties. It seems the folk do know the properties that determine the reference of names like "Jonah" and "Helen of Troy" in certain texts. What is more, we can all give a rough characterization of what scholars seeking Jonah or Helen do. They start with the token names in the texts in question and work backwards, looking for the causal origins of those tokens in the story-telling practices of the past. When they find the right kind of causal origin, they have found their man or woman. That's the methodology of books and television series devoted to asking who, if anyone, was Helen of Troy.[9] But – to labor the point – discussions of who she was aren't especially the preserve of philosophers. Or, to give an example familiar to many parents, they get asked by their children, "Did Robin Hood exist?" and, "If he existed, who was he?" They know that the answer to these questions lies in the causal origins of tokens of the name "Robin Hood," in various texts, films, and television series, and the relations of those origins to information conveyed by sentences using the name.

Our final example to bring out the point – and apologies for the mouthful that is coming – that this *information channel based on*

---

[9] I have heard it said that it is more likely that Jonah existed than that Helen of Troy did, and of course it may turn out that there is no determinate answer, in one or both cases.

conventions for transmitting information using names account of the property that determines reference is folk theory is the way sentences containing proper names assist us in known ways to navigate our world, and the effects the names have on where we end up. A person's coming across a sentence containing a name can dramatically change the probabilities of that person being at, or not at, the thing named. Someone's hearing "Sammy's is a good restaurant" increases the chance that they will be at Sammy's. Someone's reading "Chernobyl is radioactive" lowers dramatically the probability of their going to Chernobyl. Or consider a phenomenon especially familiar to academics. Reading an e-mail containing the sentence "There is an interesting conference coming up in Bielefeld" increases the probability of faculty from all over the world ending up in the one place, namely Bielefeld (an early version of some of these ideas was presented at a conference in Bielefeld).

What is the explanation? Part of the explanation has to be that we know of distinctive marks of the places in question. You keep clear of Chernobyl by knowing a property, a marker if you like, distinctive of Chernobyl, and making sure that wherever you are doesn't have that property. You get yourself to Bielefeld by knowing a marker for that city, and making sure that where you end up has that marker. Of course each of us doesn't need to use the same marker, but we each need a marker. We each need a uniquely possessed property but don't need the same one. Why do we need a *uniquely* possessed property? Suppose that the best I can do by way of pinning down Bielefeld is with a property that it shares with Berlin. Then it will be 50:50 or thereabouts whether I turn up in Bielefeld or in Berlin. But we all know that it isn't 50:50. Everyone who went to the conference in Bielefeld knew in advance that they would very likely get there, and knew that the same held for the others who set out for Bielefeld from all over the world, barring accidents.

How come we were all so confident? Certainly, many of us knew very little about Bielefeld when we first read the e-mail and were well aware, for instance, that there might be two or more cities called "Bielefeld." What we did know, however, was how to use the word "Bielefeld" to get the information we needed. We sent e-mails containing the word in sentences like "How do we get to Bielefeld?" to the organizers who sent out the original e-mail. We used the word in talking to travel agents and colleagues. And we knew that the sentences that came back to us would carry information about Bielefeld. That is to say, we exploited our knowledge that the city was the object about which these sentences carried information. And this was all common knowledge. None of us felt it necessary to send out e-mails explaining about naming practices and the way they sustain information channels in order to justify using the word "Bielefeld" to get the information we needed. True, many of us were philosophers of language, but historians and bankers are equally good at using names to get to the city where the conference they want to go to is being held.

Speaking more generally, it is common knowledge that the world is a complex place with a huge number of different objects. We often need to be able to differentiate one from another – I want my mail to get to my house and not yours – and although it is plausible that there will be some property unique to each and every object – there are no *absolutely* identical twins, for example – this fact is of little use to us if we don't know the differentiating property. Of necessity we set up systems that differentiate in known ways between objects. That's what we are doing when we name streets, cities, and people, give numbers to rooms, put the black dot on one of the two white cue balls in billiards, and so on. Often (tokens of) the names and numbers – the differentiating labels – are physically attached to the objects. For example, room numbers are typically placed on or very near the room they serve to differentiate. But there are plenty of exceptions, our relation to our own names being an obvious example. In hospital, where it is especially important that there be no confusion, we are tagged with our names – they are literally attached to us – but by and large our connection to our names is a causal one. I *answer* to my name; I *put* my name on forms. But assigning names is only a first step in differentiating objects. There are many cities called "London." How then do we ensure that a letter gets to the desired city out of, as it might be, London England and London Ontario? One way is to append the word "England" or the word "Ontario" to "London." But the most widespread way of handling the problem is to trade on our knowledge of the way people observe the convention of transmitting information using names via their causal connections to the named object. A meeting is called for room *110* next Friday. Where do I go? There are many rooms numbered *110* in my university, and maybe millions numbered *110* around the world. But I know that the person calling the meeting is observing the convention of using "*110*" to deliver information about the room in question. This in itself may answer my question. I know there is only one room *110* that stands in the kind of causal connection that would allow her to observe the convention. But if this isn't enough, I send her sentences containing "*110*" and get the detail I need from her responses, for I know that she will be observing the convention, and thus know that what will come back will likely be identifying information about the room I need to find.

What I have said in the last few paragraphs is common knowledge, folk knowledge. It is part of understanding the role of names in a natural language like ours. The property that settles the reference of a proper name isn't an unknown one. It is the kind of property Kripke talks about. My dissent from the causal theory of reference is simply my insistence that the property is no secret.

I have said things like this before; others have said things like this before.[10] We have had less impact than one (I) might have hoped. It is still conventional wisdom that the description theory of reference for proper names is false.[11] One explanation for my failure is no doubt that I did not make my points well enough. But there are four other explanations for resistance, each of more interest.

One is that many insist that the question of folk knowledge of the reference-determining property is incidental to the central question. Maybe the folk do know the property and maybe it is the property that causal theorists of reference say it is, but the key point is that a user of a name can refer to the referent of the name without knowing the property. Their claim is that user ignorance is compatible with successful reference.[12] Another reason for resistance to our defense of descriptivism is that many hold that I am wrong in insisting that the folk have knowledge of the reference-determining property. Sometimes the argument is that the folk, and highly trained philosophers if it comes to that, cannot *specify* the reference-determining property in full, exceptionless detail. What the folk have is a recognitional ability subserved by information at the sub-personal level.[13]

---

[10]   See, e.g., the papers by Kroon cited above; Evans (1982); Lewis (1999); Jackson (2005).
[11]   Thus the sentence starting "But with the demise of descriptivist theories of proper names, ..." in Tye (2009, p. 81).
[12]   See, e.g., Devitt and Sterelny (1999), and Soames (2002; 2005)
[13]   See, e.g., Davies (2004) and the response by Braddon-Mitchell (2004).

They don't have personal level knowledge of the reference-determining property. A third resistance point is that some insist that a theory of reference for names must make sense of the way quite young children refer using names, and it is hard to believe that they know about information channels sustained by naming and usage conventions. Finally (and most influentially is my impression), many hold, first, that the description theory of reference is committed to the equivalence, or the interchangeability in a range of contexts, of sentences of the form "*N* is *F*" with sentences of the form "The *D* is *F*," or maybe the "The actual *D* is *F*," or maybe "The *D* is *F*," combined with a special scope rule, where "*D*" gives the reference-determining property; and, second, that there are decisive objections to equivalence and interchangeability.[14] They are right on the second point. There *are* decisive objections to equivalence and interchangeability. But it is a mistake to hold that the description theory is committed to them, a mistake sometimes made by description theorists, it should be said. (*Mea culpa* but I wasn't alone.) We will discuss the issues raised by these four explanations for resistance in the order I have listed them.

4. What is required of a user of a name?

The objection, remember, is that though I might (*might*) be right about the reference-determining property and folk knowledge of it, a user's use (call him "Fred") of "Cicero" can refer to Cicero when Fred doesn't know the property.[15] How so? Is the idea that a certain, information-bearing causal chain from Cicero to "Cicero" in Fred's language community is, in itself, enough to make it the case that Fred's use of "Cicero" refers to Cicero, regardless of Fred's mental state? But now there is a crucial question to be asked: is the token use of "Cicero" *by Fred* part of that causal chain or not? Suppose not. Then there is a serious problem. There are very many causal chains from very many Ciceros to very many tokens of "Cicero."[16]

---

[14] See, e.g., Soames 2002; 2005a; 2005b.
[15] For versions of this line of objection see Devitt and Sterelny (1999, p. 99) and Soames (2005, p. 301).
[16] I take this point from Kroon (2009, p. 152), but please do not hold him responsible for my development of it.

Which Cicero does Fred's use of "Cicero" name? The defender of reference in the face of ignorance has no way to answer this question. Any answer will be as arbitrary as any other answer. The only way out is to include Fred's use in the causal chain. That way there will arguably be a non-arbitrary answer to the question of what his use names. It will name the same thing as its predecessors in the chain that Fred's use is a part of – say, one that goes back to Cicero, NY. But now we come up against Kripke's aardvark point. The use has to be the right use. If Fred hears the word "Cicero" used by someone to refer to Cicero, NY, and thinks it would be a good name for his aardvark, Fred isn't referring to Cicero, NY, by his consequent uses of "Cicero" despite its causal connection to a token that does refer to Cicero, NY.

What is the right kind of use? Surely, the use where Fred is following the convention of conveying information about something named in the past. The use on which, if he hears "Cicero is a fast growing city," he will repeat it, or maybe employ his knowledge of the relation between house prices and growth, to pass on putative information with the sentence "House prices in Cicero may well have held up better that those in Florida." The attempt to bracket out Fred's mind from the story about what he refers to using a name fails. It has to fail. The point was in fact clear from the moment we came across the aardvark.

It might be suggested that, although we can't leave Fred's mind out of the account of how "Cicero" in his mouth names what, if anything, it names, we do not have to suppose that he knows the linguistic conventions governing naming (which is in effect what we required above). Much less is enough. He needs merely to have the right intentions. The suggestion might be that Fred may succeed in referring to the very thing others in his community refer to when they use the name simply as a result of the name's being in public use, together with the standing intention that his use of words conform with the linguistic conventions of his community.[17] Here what must be meant is the standing intention to use words in conformity with some given *token* use or uses. Otherwise we will have the "too many referents" problem over again. There will, that is, be no answer as

---

[17] Something like this suggestion seems to be at work in Soames (2005b, p. 301, and 2007, p. 39).

to which of the many Ciceros, Fred's use of "Cicero" refers to. Let us suppose this is what Soames has in mind, and suppose further that the token use Fred has the standing intention to conform to is one that refers to Cicero, NY. There are three cases. In the first, he has no idea how his community uses the token of "Cicero" in question. In this case he won't be using the word very much. He will be like someone with the standing intention to observe the conventions of a bridge bidding system in the absence of knowing what they are. People in that situation don't do any bidding until they learn what the conventions are. The very fact they have the intention to conform means they don't act until they know, or at least have an opinion about, what it is to conform. *Mutatis mutandis* for those who seek to have their word usage conform to that of their community. In the second case, Fred is confident that the token of "Cicero" in question is used for a certain color (as some tokens of "Cicero" are, I understand). He is wrong, but that is what he thinks. His standing intention then makes him use "Cicero is attractive" just when he thinks that the color is attractive, and "Cicero is becoming more popular" just when he thinks that the color is becoming more popular. It is obvious that Fred is not referring to Cicero, NY. He is instead referring to a color. His standing intention in this case fails to bring his reference into conformity with that of his language community. In the final case, he is confident that the token in question is used as part of an information preserving chain, etc. In this case his standing intention will mean that his use of "Cicero" refers to Cicero, NY, but this will be *because he knows about the convention for using names and is following it.*

What is the moral? Intending to conform and having standing intentions to conform aren't, in the final analysis, what matter. *Conforming* is what matters. And in a way that was obvious from the start. Why seek to conform or have a standing intention to conform if *actually* conforming isn't, at the end of the day, what is crucial?

We should, however, note that there is a sense in which the emphasis the suggestion places on the role of one's language community is fully in accord with the kind of description theory I affirm on behalf of the folk. It is users' language communities, with their observance of the conventions, that underpin the informational integrity of the causal chains that run from dubbings of objects to token sentences.

Our difference is that I insist that users of the name know about the conventions and the information-preserving chains, and need to know about them, if they are to refer when they use a name. Here it is apposite to recall a passage in *Naming and Necessity*:

> In general our reference depends not just on what we think ourselves, but on other people in the community, the history of how the name reached one, and things like that. It is by following such a history that one gets to the reference. (Kripke 1980, p. 95)

My (and I am sure I speak for other causal descriptivists here) objection to this passage is restricted to Kripke's suggestion that depending on "what we think ourselves" would leave out the role of the community. The role of the community is common knowledge. It is something we think ourselves. This is clear, as we said earlier, from the way the folk follow "such a history" in seeking Helen of Troy or Robin Hood.

5. The issue about personal level knowledge

Our brains locate sounds by using the connection between the location of a sound and the out-of-phase effects at our ears when the sound reaches them (and other stuff like the differential filtering effect of the head, but we will simplify). But we don't draw conclusions about the location of a sound by knowing the out-of-phase effects at our ears and proceeding to infer the location from this knowledge. The processing is sub-personal. Something similar is true for face recognition. We rarely identify someone by noting that their face has property *P* and inferring that, as only George's face has property *P*, it must be George we are looking at; we simply recognize George's face. The recognition is undoubtedly driven by a property distinctive of his face, but the property is recorded at the sub-personal level.

There are exceptions of course. *Descriptions* of wanted persons sometimes lead to their capture. Perhaps the bulletin includes the words "the suspect has a tattoo of a rose on his left cheek and a fresh scar on his forehead," and that is enough to enable members of the public to identify the suspect. This would be a case of using personal level information to identify someone, but this is not normally how we identify our friends, or politicians on television. Try giving a list of properties of Tony Blair's face that enables someone else to identify him on television with confidence. You very likely won't be able to, but you can recognize Blair easily enough.

Is the property that determines reference like the property that underpins face recognition, something that operates at the sub-personal level? If that is right, the folk don't know the property. Their brains 'know' it if you like, but they don't. However, this suggestion can't be right.

First, if it were right, *philosophers* aren't going to find the reference-determining property. It took some physics and neuroscience to find the property that underpins our ability to locate sounds. Philosophical reflection didn't do it, and no one thought for a moment that it would. Now, we know that there is a reference-determining property – that follows from supervenience – and some philosophers claim to know what it is. That is precisely what the causal theory of reference for proper names is all about, and of course the view I am defending is a version of the causal theory with an emphasis on information-preserving channels. But if which property it is is a sub-personal matter, we should be calling in neuroscientists and cognitive psychologists. Philosophers *qua* philosophers cannot tell us, any more than the folk can. It would be a mistake in principle to think that the seminal philosophical ideas we find in *Naming and Necessity* bear on the question. This is very hard to believe.

Secondly, when we recognize in ways underpinned sub-personally, we typically need to be 'trained up' beforehand. The first time you see Tony Blair on television you won't recognize him. You need to be told that it is Tony Blair you are looking at it. You need to get the information at the personal level. *Subsequently*, you are able to recognize him without personal level cues (though they often help). Also, we are all familiar with the way our recognitional capacities are blunted by unfamiliar surroundings. Someone we recognize on the tennis court we may fail to recognize in the police station. However, our ability to find cities using sentences containing their names does not depend on being acquainted with the cities first (no 'training up' is required), and is surprisingly resilient. Indeed, one of the great strengths of our naming practices is the way they enable us to find *unfamiliar* places in *unfamiliar* situations. We find Bielefeld or 10 Elm Street despite never having been there before, and it doesn't matter much what the weather is like.

Thirdly, the key fact that tells us that an identification underpinned by the sub-personal is in fact underpinned by the sub-personal, namely, our inability to make the identification from descriptions alone, is missing in the case of finding the reference of proper names. Readers and reviewers of books or television series devoted to arguing about the identity of Helen of Troy or Robin Hood are in a position to judge whether or not the book or program succeeded in identifying Helen of Troy or Robin Hood, and, if they are undecided, this will be because either they need more information – more personal level information, that is – or because the matter is indeterminate: there is no clearly correct candidate to be the right kind of causal origin of the information carried by "Helen of Troy" or "Robin Hood" sentences in the classic texts. But the evidence offered by the books and television series is essentially in words on the page or screen, or from the mouths of those fronting the cameras. And of course I could have made essentially the same point by reference to the very literature that drives so much of the debate over the theory of reference, starting with Kripke's and Putnam's seminal contributions. The literature is full of *descriptions* of possible cases combined with invitations to make one or another judgment about what thing is referred to by some name or other. This methodology would be a nonsense if our judgments were underpinned by the sub-personal.

Finally, the importance of, for example, ending up in the right city for a conference means that it makes very good sense that we should have personal level markers for cities, and the same goes for people and the other objects we name. The rationale here is the same as that for having personal level markers for the poisons in our medicine cabinets. We make sure our children know what the skull and cross-bones on a label signifies. (We return to this issue in the second half of the final lecture.)

6. The demand for precise and explicit specifications

I said that the folk know the reference-determining property. I gave a sketch of what it was and noted its importance for the acquisition of information about objects. I supported the claim that the folk know the property by observing that, if they don't, it is strange we aren't telling them about it more vigorously given the importance of information, and by observing, moreover, that the way folk use sentences containing proper names makes it clear that they do know the property. However, I did not give a precise specification in words of the property. Some insist, or seem to insist, that any defender of the description theory must do what I did not do.[18] We mentioned Devitt and Soames in this connection. (It is perhaps worth noting that some who hold the view discussed a moment ago, the view that we don't have knowledge of the reference-determining property but do carry, at the sub-personal level, information about it, may be assuming that all personal level knowledge can be given a precise verbal expression. But this would be a mistake. Dogs and gorillas have beliefs but cannot give them precise verbal expressions. All the same, belief is a personal level state.)

A short reply on behalf of the description theory is that knowing a property and being able to give a precise specification of the property in words are two different things. But, as the issue comes up in discussion so often, the objection deserves a longer discussion. However, this longer discussion needs to be set in the context of some remarks on what a theory of reference for names is a theory *of*.

7. What is a theory of reference a theory of?

To date, we have followed the common practice of taking for granted our target notion – the reference relation between names and the things they name – and have moved straight to a discussion of the way the relation supervenes on the nature of what is named or referred to, and of the arguments against the account of the relation given by the description theory. But what, more exactly, is our target? Obviously we are talking about a word to world relation but there are many word to world relations. Which word to world relation is the one we are focused on, which is the one that has been the focus of so much discussion since Putnam's and Kripke's contributions?

---

[18] Sometimes the objection is put by saying that description theorists cannot *supply* the description; see, e.g., Devitt (forthcoming). But of course they can: "the reference-determining property for 'Plato'" is a perfectly good description.

That is to say, what is a theory of reference a theory *of*? (Thanks here to Josh Sheptow for discussion.)

Let me start with a simple distinction. I don't know the day I will die. Does this mean I don't know the reference of "the day I will die"? Yes and no. The sense in which I *don't* know the reference is that I don't know which day is the fateful day. I know it will be after today. I know it will before 2040. But if you listed the days between now and January 1, 2040 and asked me which one it is, I couldn't say (although I do not give much credence to the days near the end of that period). The sense in which I *do* know the reference is that I know what it takes to be the reference of "the day I will die." I know how a day has to be, the property it has to have, to be the day I will die. In that sense I do know the reference of "the day I will die."

Our interest in these lectures is primarily with reference in the second sense. We are concerned with the way we use words and sentences to represent things as being a certain way, or, equivalently, to give putative information about how the world is. And what it takes for x to be the referent of "the day I will die" is what we represent about how things are, the putative information we give about how things are, when we affirm "x is the day I will die." Or consider the sentence "Today is not the day I will die." If one knows what it takes to be the reference of "today" and what it takes to be the reference of "the day I will die" (and the way negation and predication work), one knows what that sentence represents about how things are. It says that the thing which has what it takes to be the referent of "today" lacks what it takes to be the referent of "the day I will die." Our interest is in the content of language in the sense tied to how sentences represent things to be, the putative information they deliver, with, as we will often abbreviate it, the *ir-content* of sentences.[19] This means that our interest in the reference of words lies in how something has to be to be the reference of a word, for it is that which feeds most directly into how sentences containing the words represent things to be, into, that is to say, their ir-content. More especially, we are interested in the contributions of names of kinds and proper names to the ir-content of a small number

---

[19]   Sometimes I will simply talk of content when the context makes clear that it is ir-content that we are discussing.

of rather simple sentences containing them – sentences like "Plato was a great philosopher," "The conference is in Bielefeld," and "Water is nearby."

In this sense of reference, the question, What is the reference of "circle"? is a boring question. Boring because we all know the answer. We all know what we are saying about how things are when we use the word "circle" to say how something is. We are saying that it is an instance of the following shape: O. To say it in terms of reference: there is a function, the reference function, that goes from "circle" to the property of being a circle (or maybe the set of circular things in logical space, or … ; the different ways of putting the same basic idea are not significant in this context), and in understanding the word "circle," we grasp that function. In this sense of "reference," there aren't many reference relations between "circle" and the world. There is just the one, the one from the word to the shape. Any other word to world relation delivers the wrong answer to be reference in the intended sense. Or better, delivers the wrong answer as far as English is concerned. There is no reason why there shouldn't be a language that uses "circle" to do the job we use "square" for, and *for that language* the reference relation we are talking about goes from "circle" to being square rather than to being round.

We will sometimes talk of the ir-content of a word, "circle," as it might be – the word, not a sentence containing the word – when it is important to bear in mind that we are talking of the reference of the word "circle" in the sense that relates most directly to its contribution to the ir-content of, say, "There are circles." In these terms, the boring question is, What is the ir-content of "circle"? However, a question that is far from boring is, How come "circle" has that content and not, say, the content that the word "square" has? Even for a simple word like "circle," the *getting* of content (reference) question, as we might call it, is challenging and controversial. The same goes *mutatis mutandis* for sentences containing the word. Saying that the ir-content of "There are circles" is that there are things with the shape – O – is unexciting, because it is so obviously true. But how that sentence comes to have the ir-content it does have is highly controversial.

It is perhaps worth taking a moment to point out that there is no significance in the fact that I have chosen to frame matters using "reference" instead of, say, "satisfaction." The key point – a point we will discuss at more length in the next lecture – is that our ability to use language to say how our world is shows that there are word to world relations we grasp, just as our ability to use the map of the London Underground to find our way across London shows that there are map to distribution of stations relations that we grasp. I have expressed what we grasp as the reference function from, e.g., "circle" to shape ○, but I could equally have said that what we grasp is that an object *satisfies* "circle" just if it has the property: shape ○. And of course there are still further ways one might express the basic idea.

I can now say what it is we are discussing when we discuss the theory of reference for names. We are discussing the role of names in making claims about how things are. I think Jason Stanley is right when he says "Suppose that Hannah utters … 'Bill Clinton lived in Arkansas' … Hannah imparts certain information about the world" (2007, p. 5). To say it in the jargon of representation, by uttering "Bill Clinton lived in Arkansas," Hannah represents, correctly as it happens, that things are a certain way; that's the (putative) information she imparts. Mostly, in the interest of keeping things as simple as possible, we will focus on sentences of a simple subject-predicate form. So for us the question, What is a theory of reference for proper name "N"? is in effect the question, What is the contribution of "N" to how "N is F" represents things to be, to the putative information the sentence delivers?

From this perspective, the debate over the right theory of reference for names is the debate over the contribution that names make to how things are being represented to be. It is over their contribution to the informational value of sentences containing them. The version of the description theory I have been defending says that their contribution is to be parts of information channels. By way of contrast, one version of the direct reference theory would say that the contribution of names is to pick out their referent and *that's it*. This kind of direct reference theory typically allows that there is such a thing as the reference-determining property, and it may or may not allow that the folk know what it is, and the property may or may not be as a version of the causal theory of reference says it is, but what the theory holds firm to is that the property in question is not part of the content. Instead it is the content determiner. In terms of the distinction alluded to a little while ago, the answer to the question, What is the content of "N"? is that it is some object o, whereas the answer to the question, How come "N" has content o? is in terms of the property.[20] One version of this kind of direct reference theory says that "Plato" has the content Plato, and the reason why it has that content is that Plato and "Plato" stand in a certain causal, information-bearing relationship.

We can now see what is wrong with the objection that supporters of the description theory have not specified the relevant property with due precision. One thing is clear. We *are* able to describe the world using words. We can say what things are *like* using words. Why am I so upset when I hear the word "terminal" in connection with a disease I have? Because I know the property being ascribed (for I know what it takes for "terminal" to apply to something), and it is one I don't welcome. Why were Democrats so pleased to hear the words "Obama has won" uttered on television on the night of November 4, 2008? Because they knew the property being ascribed, and it was one they welcomed. Why do we bother saying things like "Sweden is a liberal society"? Because we know what we are saying about Sweden and it is something worth saying. Our ability to describe the world using words is a datum.

This means that for some (*some*) words it is a datum that the description theory is true. There are words that we know apply to x just if x has a given property.[21] However, it is not possible to give a precise expression in words of what it takes to be a liberal society. We can say some useful things, and often do so when we explain to our children what makes for a liberal society. Having a free press is important, as is having a right to vote that operates in a way that gives more than one party some chance of winning, whereas a

---

[20]   Stalnaker has been as clear as anyone I know in putting this kind of position, see, e.g., (2003a).

[21]   I know philosophers of language sometimes seem to be denying this. They produce sentences like "The reference of a word 'W' is not settled by known properties P_1, P_2, etc. Whether 'W' refers to x is always a matter involving best theory and maybe selectional history," in a way that might suggest this is a thesis for words across the board. But this would not be the right way to read them, for two reasons. First, they use the words "P_1" and "P_2" in a way that presupposes that we do know the reference of those words. In expressing the view that certain properties don't settle reference, they perforce use *words* for precisely those very properties. Secondly, there would be no point in using terms like "best theory" and "selectional history" unless they and their readers knew which properties had to be instantiated in order for those terms to apply.

country's being cold in the winter is in itself neither here nor there. What is more, we can say that someone who looks for the property of being a liberal society as if it were something separate from having a free press, equality before the law, and so on is confused. Being a liberal society is a matter of some suitable combination of equality before the law, the right to vote, and so on. It isn't an extra feature that somehow, mysteriously 'goes along with' equality before the law, the right to vote, and so on. However, it is notorious that we cannot write down a precise list of necessary and sufficient conditions for being a liberal society. Opinions differ as to why this is impossible and about its significance, but there is consensus that it is impossible.[22]

The same point can be made with terms for shapes. For some shapes we know the formula. The word "circle" applies to a shape just if it is a closed plane figure, each point of which is equidistant from a fixed point. In that sense we can give the description or property that determines its reference. However, there are shape terms for which this isn't possible. Those who can read print and handwriting in the Roman alphabet have at their disposal the term "an a." It applies to the relevant commonality between: a, a, A, A, ... Its reference goes by description: it applies to something just if it is of relevant qualitative kind. We know what the kind is. This isn't a case of sub-personal knowledge. When someone scrutinizes a sample of handwriting and declares a certain configuration to be an a, you know at the personal level – you know, that is, in the ordinary sense of "know" – what they are saying about how the configuration is. But we cannot give a neat set of rules for when a shape is an a. This is one reason it is hard to program computers to read handwriting (and printouts in non-standard fonts). Or think of the knowledge one gets from perception. Perception often yields knowledge about the distribution of *properties*, but our ability to put that knowledge into words is limited.

The moral is that we should not demand that supporters of a description theory of reference for a word, "W," give what is in effect a reductive analysis of the property they hold determines the reference of "W." They must be able to give a reasonable indica-

---

[22]   For one opinion about why it is impossible and its relative insignificance, see Jackson (forthcoming a).

tion of the property in words – as we did for being a liberal society, and for being part of an information channel – and it is important that we can recognize cases by the descriptions given of them, but that is possible for the reference of both "is a liberal society" and "Gödel."

I guess, to put it in slogan form, the point I'm making is, beware the old double standard.

8. In the mouths of the very young

Very young children parrot our words. Sometimes they do more than parrot them; they repeat them with some degree or other of understanding. All the same, it would be strange to make their use of a word a major constraint on a theory about *our* use of it. It would be like insisting that what an expert means by "RAM" has to conform to what I mean by it. But something awfully like this does seem to be going on in the objection to the description theory of reference that runs somewhat as follows: very young children refer to Paris when they use the word "Paris" as in, say, "Mummy and Daddy are in Paris," but it is obviously wrong to credit them with a grasp of the kind of causal information-preserving property that I have suggested determines the reference of "Paris." But as this objection comes up so often in discussion, it calls for a more extended discussion.[23]

How very young children represent the world to be when they use various words is more a subject for child psychologists than philosophers. All the same, parents and grandparents can have empirical information that bears on the subject, and when they do, it can count *against* the view that very young children refer to the same things we do when they repeat our words. Here is a case in point. One of my young grandchildren has a small dog called "Oskar." She says "Oskar" when she sees him. I might have thought she was using it as a name for Oskar until I was told that she says "Oskar" in the presence of any small dog. Empirical evidence relating to word usage is very much to the point when considering the question of whether and when children are using a name, or indeed any word, as we do.

---

[23]   My discussion here draws on helpful discussion at the University of Vermont.

We note above the evidence that tells us that we – the mature folk, those of us who know what is going on when we search for the Jonah of the Bible, or Helen of Troy, or Robin Hood, or Bielefeld – are using proper names as parts of information channels. To the extent that some child isn't using a proper name in that kind of way, they are not using the name as we do.

The upshot is that the objection to the description theory from the word usage of very young children faces a destructive dilemma. Either they use, say, "Paris," as we do, in which case we should credit them with a grasp of the information-preserving causal chain, or else they don't use the word as we do, in which case their usage is irrelevant to the right theory of *our* use. Perhaps those who advance the objection from very young children are implicitly supposing that a child's *trying* to use a word as we do is the same as their using a word as we do, but we saw the problems with this kind position earlier (in §4 above).

9. The description theory and interchangeability

I now come to what I heralded as the most influential reason for rejecting the description theory of reference for names. It comes up again and again, in one form or another, in the writings of opponents of the description theory.[24]

Suppose, runs the objection, that the description theory is correct for proper name "N." This means that there is a property, being D, that determines the reference of "N," and that this is known by competent users of the name. Then "N" will refer to x if and only if x is the D, and competent users of "N" know this. Then "N is F" will mean the same as, or be equivalent in some strong sense to, "The D is N." But there are decisive arguments against the equivalence of "N is F" with "The D is F," for any "D" that might plausibly be the reference-determining property.

The last claim is correct. There *are* decisive arguments against the equivalence. The problem with the objection is that the description theory is not committed to the equivalence. Despite the allure

---

[24]   Soames (2002; 2005a) are prime examples.

of the argument to the conclusion that description theorists are committed to the equivalence – indeed, the *a priori* equivalence – of "*N* is *F*" with "The *D* is *F*," for some "*D*," and despite the fact that description theorists sometimes hold that they are so committed, they aren't.

The easiest way to see this is to reflect on sentences of the form: "I am *F*." There is no mystery about the reference rule for "I" in such sentences. The rule is that it refers to the producer of the sentence. There may, in some cases, be a certain amount of argy-bargy about how to spell out what it takes to be the producer of the sentence. I encourage Fred to run for office. As a result Fred says, when nominations are called, "I am a candidate." I caused the sentence to be uttered but I am not the producer in the relevant sense. Fred is, and the token of "I" refers to Fred and not to me. Anyone who has wrestled with the problem of deviant causal chains will suspect that it may not be easy to say exactly why, in this example, Fred counts as the producer of the sentence and so as the referent of the token of "I" whereas I don't.[25] All the same, the reference rule is straightforward. "I" refers to the producer of the sentence. What is occasionally tricky is saying why one person counts as the producer whereas another is a causal factor but not the producer.[26]

This means that a description theory is correct for tokens of "I" in "I am *F*." The reference of "I" goes by, is determined by, whatever has the property of being the producer of the token sentence. And that is common knowledge and part of what it is to understand how "I" works. This is fully in accord with our approach to the question, What is a theory of reference a theory of? The information imparted by, how things are being represented to be by, an assertoric use of "I am *F*," is that the producer of the sentence is *F*, and someone who does not know this has a defective grasp of how "I" works in this kind of sentence in English.

---

[25] For evidence for the intractability of saying wherein deviance lies, see, e.g., Davidson (1980).

[26] There is also the complication posed by cases where one person produces a token of "I" and another completes the sentence. A reader pointed out that in such cases the "I" may refer to the person who produces the "I," not the person who completes the sentence. But that is not always the case. Consider a survey asking one to complete "I admire ... ." The token of "I" in this case does not refer to the writer of the survey but to the person who completes the sentence.

However, it would be a mistake to hold that "I am *F*" is equivalent to "The producer of 'I am *F*' is *F*," as is widely acknowledged. "I have a beard" is not equivalent to "The producer of 'I have a beard' has a beard." There may be, indeed no doubt are, many producers of the sentence "I have a beard," and even if there weren't, someone who says "I have a beard" isn't saying *inter alia* that there is only one producer of "I have a beard."[27] True, there is only one producer of the token sentence, but that doesn't help. "The producer of the *token* of 'I have a beard' has a beard" faces the same problem. There will be many tokens. It may well be that there is some unique specification of the token in question. But there is no plausibility whatever to the suggestion that "I have a beard" is equivalent to something like "The producer of the token of 'I have a beard' at noon, November 15, 2007, in New York, at 365 Fifth Ave, has a beard." That kind of detail is no part of how I represent things to be when I use "I have a beard."

It would be even more obviously a mistake to hold that the sentence "Fred believes that I have beard" is equivalent to "Fred believes that the producer of the sentence 'I have a beard' has a beard." Perhaps Fred believes that I have a beard but that I never ever comment on the fact and, moreover, that there is only one person in existence who ever produces the sentence "I have a beard" and that person is, according to Fred, mistaken on the point (they don't have a beard). In that case "Fred believes that I have beard" is true, whereas "Fred believes that the producer of the sentence 'I have a beard' has a beard" is false. Or perhaps I am clean shaven and Fred knows it but thinks (no doubt mistakenly) that there is only one person in existence who ever produces the sentence "I have a beard" and Fred believes this person is bearded. In that case "Fred believes that I have beard" is false, whereas "Fred believes that the producer of the sentence 'I have a beard' has a beard" is true.

The moral is that the question of whether the reference of a singular term, "*T*," goes by a known property, being *D*, when knowledge of this fact is part of understanding the term, is a distinct

---

[27]   There are, of course, more reasons than this one to deny the equivalence. When I believe that I have a beard and give voice to it using the sentence "I have a beard," the content of my belief has a lot in common with the content of my sentence but the belief is not about a sentence. But one decisive reason is enough for our purposes here.

question from the question whether "*T* is *F*" is equivalent to "The *D* is *F*."

We might have argued that "I have a beard" isn't equivalent to "The producer of 'I have a beard' has a beard" by pointing out that "I" is a rigid designator whereas "The producer of 'I have a beard' " isn't, thus reprising an issue that looms large in the debate over the description theory of reference. But that would invite the thought that it might be possible to hold that "I" is equivalent to "the *actual* ... ." This would be a mistaken thought. The reason we gave for holding that "I have a beard" is not equivalent to "The producer of 'I have a beard' has a beard" had nothing to do with the difference in respect to rigidity. The message in what is to come in later lectures is that it is a mistake *in principle* to hold that sentences of the form "*N* is *F*" are equivalent to "The *D* is *F*," and to think one might restore equivalence by rigidifying, or by imposing a special scope reading, is to fail to grasp the fundamental reason why the equivalence fails. All the same, the description theory of reference for proper names is true. The reference of proper names does go by known properties, and knowing what the properties are is part of understanding the role of proper names in representing that the world is thus and so, in passing on or imparting putative information that the world is thus and so.

I am doing a certain amount of 'territory marking' here. One might insist that *by definition* the description theory of proper names holds that "*N* is *F*" is equivalent to "The *D* is *F*," for some *D*, in some strong sense, with special clauses to do with rigidity or scope added. Indeed, critics of the description theory sometimes write as if it was constitutive of the description theory that "*N* is *F*" is *a priori* equivalent to "The *D* is *F*," for some *D*. If one does so insist, then I am with the majority in repudiating the description theory of reference for proper names. But then I (and we) will need another label for the theory of proper names I defend. I hereby stipulate that what I mean by the description theory is the theory I have been defending above.

10. What is to come and a final objection noted

I can now highlight a major item on the agenda of the lectures to come. I say above that, despite the fact that the reference of proper names goes by known properties and that knowing what the properties are is part of understanding the role of proper names in representing that the world is thus and so, sentences of the form "N is F" are not equivalent to sentences of the form "The D is F," and that this is so for reasons that have nothing especially to do with the familiar issues about rigidity and scope. How can this be correct? We will be saying how. The story starts in the next lecture, but I will finish this lecture by addressing an objection many will, I suspect, be itching to make around about now.

We noted earlier the distinction between the content a sentence in fact has versus how it comes to have that content, and the correlative distinction between the reference a term in fact has versus how it comes to have that reference. The first concerns how things are being represented to be by a sentence and the contribution a word makes to what we are calling its ir-content, whereas the second concerns how the sentence comes to have the ir-content it does have and how a word comes to make the contribution that it does make to that ir-content. The objection is that when I said that the reference rule for "I" in "I am F" is that "I" refers to the producer of the token sentence, what I said was true *only* if I was talking about how "I" comes to have the reference it does. In the sense of "reference" tied to the contribution "I" makes to how, say, "I have a beard" represents things to be, runs the objection, the correct answer concerning the reference of "I" is a Millian one. That is, if Frank Jackson says "I have a beard," the content is Frank Jackson's having a beard – that very person's having a beard; something we might represent with the ordered couple <FJ, having a beard>. In this sense of "content," the content of "I have a beard" varies depending on who says it, and the variation in content is tracked by the reference rule we are discussing.

We will discuss this issue in more detail in Lecture Three, but let me give the short version of my reply here. The informational value of "I have a beard" does *not* depend on knowing who said it. Consider an amnesia sufferer waking in hospital with no idea of who they are. On feeling the beard on his face he knows how to say what he has just learnt – use the sentence "I have a beard." It does not matter that he does not know who he is. And someone competent in English who hears the sentence but has no idea who said it (perhaps they are out in the hospital corridor) knows what is been said and gets information from hearing the sentence. What information? We all know the answer to that question: the information that the person who uttered the sentence has a beard. Ergo, the reference rule we have been talking about delivers reference in the sense of its role in how things are being represented to be, its role of delivering putative information about how things are.

Lecture Two

Understanding, Representation, Information

1. Some stage setting on the value of understanding words and plans

We talked in the first lecture about the way sentences represent that things are thus and so, and are, thereby, putative sources of information. Or at least they are putative sources of information for those who know how the sentences represent things to be, for those who know the ir-contents of the sentences – to say it in our jargon. In this lecture I will set these commonplaces (it is hardly news that sentences provide putative information) in a theoretical framework.

I think of much of the lecture as a set of preliminary notes that will help us see things more clearly in later lectures, and that what I say is pretty much folk theory dressed in some philosophers' terminology. My aim is to explicate a theory that, it seems to me, lies behind the way the folk (you, me, the man or woman on the Clapham omnibus, ...) use words and sentences each and every day of our lives to acquire and provide information about our world. It may be, as Hanjo Glock suggested to me, that what I say is close to Wittgenstein's picture theory of meaning in the *Tractatus*. I won't, however, pursue that scholarly question here.[1]

Where to start? As I seek to show that what is on offer is folk theory dressed in philosophers' terminology, we need to start with something as commonsensical as possible. That might be thought to recommend starting with the notion of the facts or a fact. When we make claims about how things are using language, we seek to get the

[1] But see the discussion in Rumfitt (2005, p. 445) of Wittgenstein (1922, §4.024).

facts right, and what we say is true just if we succeed. It is often said that the folk are covert correspondence theorists, and some say that "corresponds to the facts" is pretty much a synonym for being true in the mouths of the folk. Against this, my hunch is that the folk find "the facts" as troublesome as do many philosophers. The folk come across objects, know that they have various properties, know that they stand in various relationships to each other, and that some objects are made up of other objects. Facts, however, have escaped their attention. Of course the folk do say things like "Give me the facts." But what they want is not a gift of something called "the facts." What they want is a sentence that tells things as they are – "Tell it as it is!," as interjectors at political rallies put it; "Tell it like it is," as the title of the song by George Davis and Lee Diamond has it. That is to say, the concepts the folk do have in their armory are those of things being a certain way, of things being as they are said to be by some person or sentence, and, by extension, of things being as some thinker takes them to be. Moreover, when the folk ask how things are, as in the question, How is the weather where you are? they know that there are a number of possibilities with regard to the weather, a number of ways the weather might be, and seek to know which one is how things in fact are. That is, the folk have in their armory the concept of the way things *might* be, as well as the way they in fact are.

What is more, the folk agree on the value of understanding a language. It is akin to being able to read house plans. When a couple planning their next home discuss the various possibilities with their builder over a kitchen table covered with plans, the plans are of value inasmuch as the parties are able to read them in the sense of knowing how a house would have to be to conform to a given plan. The discussions aren't about the plans as such, but about the houses that would and would not be in accord with them. When a plan gets discarded, what is ruled out is having a house that fits the plan (not quite – hard to read and badly drawn plans also get discarded). But the discussions between the builder and the couple could use sentences in place of plans, or, as typically happens, a mixture of plans and sentences. In these cases, the constraint that needs to be met is that the sentences be ones the parties to the discussion understand, and what explains the utility of using sentences in these discussions is that the parties to the discussion know how things would have to be in order to be in accord with the sentences, or in accord with the combinations of sentences and plans.

The message is that, in the same way that the value of being able to read plans rests on knowing how things would have to be to be in accord with the plans, the value of understanding a language rests on knowing how things would have to be to be in accord with sentences in the language. The Woody Allen movie *Deconstructing Harry* (1997) contains the line, "The most beautiful words in the English language are not 'I love you', but 'It's benign'." Those words are only beautiful for those who understand English, and for those who do, the beauty comes from their knowledge of how things have to be in order to be in accord with those words.

We could stipulate that understanding a sentence – when it is one of the many sentences that play the kind of representational role plans play – is knowing how things have to be in order to be in accord with the sentence. This would leave open the extent to which we understand any given word or sentence of some language we speak in a more everyday sense of understand – the one on which at least some non-experts are said to understand, to one degree or another, the word "quark," or the sentence "The development of collateralized debt obligations was a mistake." But what is anyway clear is that English speakers understand, in the stipulated sense, to some substantial extent a great many words and sentences of English. They agree about how things are being represented to be using those words and sentences, as we'll say it. If that were not the case, English would not be the marvelous communication medium for English speakers and writers that it manifestly is. (The same goes for Russian etc., but English is the language we are using and focusing on.)

To what extent would such a stipulation reflect our ordinary understanding of understanding? Some take the message of Putnam's division of linguistic labor (Putnam 1975) to be that very little is needed to count as using some word with the same meaning as one's language community. That isn't the lesson I take from his doctrine. I think we have to do some serious work to understand "quark"; simply borrowing the word is not enough. If it was enough, why do the borrowers seem so keen to learn more, and why do they lament their ignorance? Of course, borrowing is enough for co-reference in the sense of reference we distinguished from the notion of reference most closely tied to ir-content in Lecture One. If I borrow "quark" from the experts in my community – something I can do without knowing who the experts are or much about what they mean by the word – I will co-refer with the experts. I will be using "quark" for whatever the experts use "quark" for – whoever precisely they are and whatever precisely they use the word for – which is what a quark is in the language of the experts. But how I represent things to be using "quark" won't be how they represent things to be using "quark." I will be like someone who borrows "prime number" from mathematicians in a way that ensures that the term in their, the borrower's, mouth refers to 2, 3, 5, 7, etc. but who hasn't a clue, or much of a clue, about what it takes to be a prime number. Or think of someone who uses "square root of *n*" for the number that appears opposite *n* in a table of square roots. They may have no idea of what a square root is.

I know many disagree with these sentiments. The communal nature of language means, they say, that I and the experts represent alike when I borrow from the experts. I invite my opponents to think about house plans. What would they say about a builder who claimed to understand house plans but was totally unable to build a house in accord with some set of plans, despite being given all the needed resources, and who could not say, of various houses built by others, whether or not they were in accord with the plans in question, despite having good eyesight and being allowed to examine the houses in detail? Surely the right thing to say is that the builder cannot read house plans, and surely my opponents would hardly be reassured when he told them about his close links with, and deference toward, an association of master builders who were able to build and to recognize houses that conformed to the plans.

Be all this as it may, what is crucial for what is to come is the contention that very often we *do* understand sentences in the stipulated sense, in the sense that we know how things would have to be to be as the sentences represent things to be. In saying this, I may be going against some things that Williamson has said recently, and as his remarks are in part expressions of disagreement with things I have said in the past, I will take a moment to set what I am saying in the context of his remarks. I trust this will make my position clearer.

2. Agreement and shared understandings

Williamson argues that we should be liberal about the extent of the agreement needed for successful communication using a shared language.

> A complex web of interactions and dependences can hold a linguistic or conceptual practice together even in the absence of a common creed that all participants at all times are required to endorse. ...
>
> Evidently, much of the practical value of a language consists in its capacity to facilitate communication between agents in epistemically asymmetric positions, when the speaker or writer knows about things about which the hearer or reader is ignorant, perhaps mistaken. Although disagreement is naturally easier to negotiate and usually more fruitful against a background of extensive agreement, it does not follow that any particular agreement is needed for disagreement to be expressed in given words. A practical constraint on useful communication should not be confused with a necessary condition for literal understanding. (2007, p. 125)

And a little before this quotation he says:

> The idea that a shared understanding of a word requires a shared stock of platitudes depends on the assumption that uses of a word by different agents or at different times can be bound together into a common practice of using that word with a given meaning only by an invariant core of beliefs. But that assumption amounts to one of the crudest and least plausible answers to the question of what makes a unity out of diversity. In effect, it assumes that what animates a word is a soul of doctrine. (Ibid., p. 123)

What is crucial here is what Williamson means by agreement and disagreement. Shared understanding of words – giving words the same meanings – is certainly possible in the face of substantial disagreement *about how the world is*. But substantial disagreement about how things have to be in order to be as the words and sentences say they are is another matter altogether. The second is what we need substantial agreement on and is that which we typically have. You may use "Australia will not win the next Test" to say how you take things to be; I may use "Australia will win the next Test." That's no bar in itself to successful communication of how we take things to be. The problems will start if what it takes to win as you use "win" differs from what it takes to win as I use "win." The unity we need, the "invariance" we need, is on that question, not on the question of who will win. Or better, we can tolerate a degree of variance, a lack of unity, provided we know it does not matter in practice. We will discuss this second point in a bit of detail when we talk about different ways people might use the word "water" in Lecture Five.

Are Williamson and I disagreeing? I am insisting that a necessary condition for you and me to have a shared understanding of the word "win" is that what it takes to be the referent of the word is the same for both of us. Or take the term "prime number." Some use the term for any natural number exactly divisible by itself and one alone. Others use it for any natural number exactly divisible by itself and one alone, with the exception of one. The second use is its use by mathematicians and in that sense is the correct use, but I have met folk who use the term the first way. The two groups do not have a shared understanding of "prime number," despite the fact that there no doubt exists, to quote from Williamson, "a complex web of inter-actions and dependences" uniting the linguistic practices of the two groups. So, if Williamson is urging that shared understanding is possible in the face of disagreement over how things are, there is no disagreement between us; if he is urging that there does not need to be any single thing in common between people who have a shared understanding of a term in order to make "unity out of diversity," there is disagreement between us. There is, I hold, some-thing that has to be in common, namely, what it takes to fall under the term.

3. Davidson's challenge to representation

I always hope that when I say the kind of things I have just been saying, it will sound "run of the mill." But I know that some philoso-phers repudiate the representational picture of language that lies behind much of what I have said to date in this lecture and, if it comes to that, a lot of what I said in the first lecture. An example is Donald Davidson. He sees the representational picture of language as tied to the correspondence theory of truth, and sees that as reason enough to reject the representational picture. Here is a passage from Davidson:

> The correct objection to correspondence theories is ... that such theories
> fail to provide entities to which truth vehicles (whether we take these to
> be statements, sentences, or utterances) can be said to correspond. As I
> once put it, "Nothing, no *thing*, makes our statements true." If this is right,
> and I am convinced it is, we ought also to question the popular assumption
> that sentences, or their spoken tokens, or sentence-like entities, or configu-
> rations in our brains can properly be called "representations," since there
> is nothing for them to represent. If we give up facts as entities that make
> sentences true, we ought to give up representations at the same time, for
> the legitimacy of each depends on the legitimacy of the other. (2001,
> p. 184)

What can I say in reply? The first thing to say is that if the worry is
all to do with the strangeness of facts, then we are in agreement. The
folk theory sketched above does not appeal to facts. Indeed, it was
introduced with remarks about how mysterious facts are. However,
I appealed to ways things are and to ways things might be in outlining the folk theory. My suspicion is that they would be found as
objectionable as facts.

The second thing I can do by way of reply is highlight how contrary to commonsense the denial of representation is. The argument
Davidson gives for saying that sentences, for example, do not represent would apply equally to subway maps and diagrams of chess
positions. But those who look at the chess diagrams in books on great
games of the past, or who use the map of the London Underground
to find their way across London, take it for granted that what they
have in their hands represents, as it might be, a certain position at a
certain stage of the final game in the 1972 Fischer-Spassky World
Chess Championship match, or where the stations on the Central
Line are. The same goes for those who design the diagrams and maps.
It would seem bizarre for philosophers to write and tell the users and
the designers of their error. Moreover, the point about representation
underlies how the maps and diagrams give us information, and it
seems undeniable that maps and diagrams give information. Equally,
it seems undeniable that Davidson himself, in the passage quoted
above, is giving us information – information about his views. How
could this be unless his words represent how he takes things to be in
regard to the issue on the table?

Finally, I should address Davidson's objection to talk of "making
true." My impression is that what at bottom animates Davidson's
objection to thinking of sentences (and brain configurations, etc.) as

representations is that it is part of a package that thinks of sentences as *being made true* by something or other. This is why I said above that I suspect he would find "ways things are" and "ways things might be" as objectionable as facts. They are part and parcel of the making-true way of thinking about language; the way of thinking that holds, as it might be, that "It is raining outside" is made true by how things are outside. Now it is certainly true that the making true way of thinking can be developed in ways that move it outside the realm of relatively uncontroversial folk theory. Do we, for example, need for each true sentence a *dedicated* truth maker? The answer to that question is highly controversial. But we need to distinguish the status of some basic insight from the status of the various ways it might be developed by philosophers.[2] If we don't, everything just about will be in doubt. We will commit the "development fallacy," as we might tag it. Here is how it goes. Take an idea, *I*, to which we give, say, 99.9 percent credence. Ten philosophers develop it in ten mutually exclusive, jointly exhaustive ways $I_1, ..., I_{10}$, each of which has, as it might be, just under 10 percent chance of being right. The fallacy is to infer that the original idea has only 10 percent credence.

What we need for our purposes is the non-controversial core of the making-true idea. I am wondering if it is raining outside. A trusted observer goes outside and on returning utters, "It is raining outside." I know how things have to be to be as she represents them to be. That is how I get the needed information, and if things are that way, the sentence is true. The core idea is as simple as that.

4. Are we confusing semantics and pragmatics?

One way to attack the theory I have been articulating on behalf of the folk is to attack its commitment to representationalism about language. That is the attack coming from Davidson. Another way is to question the connection between understanding and representation. Of course, one might say, language represents. That is undeniable. That is why we need a truth conditional account of meaning in which reference relations between words, on the one

---

[2]   For some of these ways and references, see Beebee and Dodd (2005).

hand, and the world, and objects and properties in the world, on the other hand, are center stage. However, the connection to information and to understanding is quite another matter. One can understand a sentence and the words that make it up without knowing how things have to be for them to be as the sentence represents them to be, and the meaning of a word or a sentence is to be distinguished from the information that using the word or sentence passes around. Meaning, reference, and truth belong to semantics, whereas understanding and information belong to the pragmatics of language.[3]

This kind of view is sometimes exampled using natural kind terms. Before we knew that water is H_2O, we understood the word "water" and used it to pass around information, but, runs the contention, we did not know how things had to be for them to be as "There is water nearby" represents them to be. Knowing that required discovering that water is H_2O. This is the message of externalism about reference and content. I will address the issues as they arise with natural kind terms in Lecture Three and again in Lecture Five. Here I simply want to make two points. One is a point about internal consistency.

Soames has recently argued that very little is required to count as being competent with the word "water":

> ... an otherwise competent English speaker is counted as a competent user of the word, if he or she knows that *water* is a term that stands for some natural kind that determines its extension at different world-states – even if one doesn't have any reliable way of describing that kind, other than the kind the word stands for in English. Perhaps one also has to have some idea of what type of kind it is – i.e. that it has something to do with physically constitutive characteristics – and that the stuff in question sometimes comes in liquid form. (2005b, pp. 183–4)

I would set higher standards for being a competent user of "water." Suppose I said the following about what is required to be competent with the word "cancer":

---

[3]   The most forceful presentation of a view of this kind I know is in Lalor (1997) where he talks of "... the corrupting nature of a key presupposition of Frege's framework – that semantics must account for the 'cognitive significance' of language" (p. 67) and says, near the end, "accounting for the cognitive significance of language becomes the job of the psychologist of knowledge, and *not* that of the semanticist" (p. 85).

... an otherwise competent English speaker is counted as a competent user of the word, if he or she knows that *cancer* is a term that stands for some natural kind that determines its extension at different world-states – even if one doesn't have any reliable way of describing that kind, other than the kind the word stands for in English. Perhaps one also has to have some idea of what type of kind it is – i.e. that it has something to do with physically constitutive characteristics – and that the kind in question sometimes comes in terminal form.

If I said that, I would rightly be criticized for divorcing competence with "cancer" from knowing its informational role in English. It is true of "cancer" and "water" alike that they play key roles in our language community in passing on information about how things are, and being competent with them requires knowing the information in question.[4] However, what is most important here is not this disagreement but what is presumed in the passage from Soames. He clearly thinks, and he is right in thinking this, that readers of this passage who are competent with English – and they will be the vast majority of those who read his book – know what he is saying. But what is involved in knowing what he is saying? Knowing how things would have to be to be as he says they are. What is more, he obviously hopes that a good number of his readers will go on to hold that this is in fact how things are. Whatever philosophers of language may say about one or another word in particular, they presume – rightly and inevitably – that those competent with the language their books and papers are written in, those who understand the language their books and papers are written in, know how things would have to be to be as these authors say they are, and, moreover, the authors hope that many readers will go on and hold that things are in fact that way.

Well, as so often, it is not quite that simple. There are misunderstandings, failures to put things together aright, and misreadings of various kinds. All the same, publishing papers and books in a given language makes available, in principle and very often in practice, to readers who understand the language, how things would have to be in order to be as the papers and books say they are. It is internally inconsistent for philosophers who publish and read papers to

[4] In Lecture Five I survey the plausible options for the information we pass on using the word "water".

downplay the informational value of understanding a language *across the board*.

Now for the second point. We need to do more than laud the informational value of understanding a language. We need to acknowledge that understanding a language typically allows us to extract detailed information in a way that tells us that, in understanding a language, we grasp a function that goes from words and sentences to how things are being represented to be. Sometimes, those who group meaning, representation, and truth conditions under the banner of *semantics*, and place information and understanding under the banner of *pragmatics*, implicitly downgrade the information side of the story about language. They seem to think of a sentence's meaning and truth conditions as relatively precise matters – *relatively*, as all agree that there is indeterminacy – whereas the information provided is highly context-dependent.[5] This is part of what they have in mind when they talk of information as belonging to pragmatics. Indeed, the idea seems to be that, whereas it is fine to talk of *the* meaning of a sentence or word, informational value is too vague, context-dependent, and variable between speakers for it to be sensible to talk of *the* informational value. When we hear or read a sentence we understand, "The coffee is brewed," say, there are many bits of information that we might acquire – for example, that someone is speaking, that someone desires to communicate with us, that the coffee is brewed, that someone is an English speaker, that someone wants us to have coffee with them, and so on, but there is nothing that can sensibly be called the information, in some privileged sense, that comes from the token sentence when used assertorically. By contrast, there will typically be such a thing as *the* meaning and *the* truth conditions that the sentence has.

Let me explain why I think that no view like this can possibly be correct. First, there is (again) a point about internal consistency. In arguing for the view that there is no such thing as *the* information provided by some utterance, it is taken for granted that those hearing or reading the argument know *the* information that "someone is speaking," "someone desires to communicate with us," "the coffee is brewed," "someone is an English speaker," "someone wants us to

---

[5]   See, for example, the discussion of the relation between information and semantic content at 66f. and 74f. in Soames (2002).

have coffee with them," respectively, convey. Soames, in the course of warning us against an unduly "naive view of the relationship between assertion, semantic content, and conveyed information" (2002, p. 73) details at length "the different types of information that an utterance may carry" (ibid., p. 86; he is especially concerned with utterances containing proper names). But for each different type of information, Soames uses English words that make up utterances to illustrate the type.[6] Indeed, how else could he give the needed illustrations?

Secondly, the most important thing about language is its informational value. Anyone reading the directions to a football game, waiting anxiously for the doctor's verdict, or struggling with the instructions for an item of furniture that came in a flat pack knows this. Strange it would be if what is most important is vague and radically context-dependent, whereas meaning, thought of as something separate, is precise and amenable to theory.

Thirdly, anyone who hears "The land mine is five cms from your left foot," or "It's benign," knows very well what the (*the*) informational value is. The same goes for philosophers and our books and articles. We may fail to get our message across but there is such a thing as *the* message we are seeking to get across.

Finally and perhaps most importantly, there is a general point about extracting information. You cannot get reliable information from the random, from the patternless. It is undeniable that we get detailed, reliable information about our world from coming across sentences we understand. This means we must grasp the patterned connection between words and sentences, on the one hand, and ways the world might be, on the other. That's the core around which our ability to extract the information more generally is built. Otherwise we would be in a kind of "Garbage in, garbage out" situation.

Of course, we should grant that representation in some inclusive sense is cheap. Any physical structure, including sentence tokens, will represent that so and so, for many values of so and so. The position of the pointer on a petrol gauge represents *inter alia* the level of petrol in the tank, the distance before a refuel is needed, the orientation of the motor controlling the pointer, and so on and so forth. A red flag

---

[6]   Strictly speaking, he uses sentences; no doubt in spoken presentations he used utterances in the strict sense.

represents danger but equally it will represent which way the wind is blowing. Whenever we have a function from structures that can be in various states to ways things might be, we have representation – maybe boring examples of no special interest to anyone, but examples of representation all the same.[7] But we are good at picking out the intended representation relation, and hence the intended informational or representational content, in any given situation. If someone asks what the reading on some gauge represents, we usually know which of the many possible answers is the one sought in the context. In particular, we are good at picking out the intended sense of representation on which it is true that a token of "Whales are the largest mammals" represents that whales are the largest mammals, although that token will also represent the ambient temperature (as the temperature of the token sentence will co-vary with the ambient temperature).[8]

What rules do we follow to get the right (intended) answer? It is no easy matter to say. Obviously it has a great deal to do with the intentions of the speaker but, as H. P. Grice points out, those intentions will include doing some communicating, and that is not what the sentence represents in the sense we are concerned with.[9] When I say "There is water due east," I intend to communicate something important, but I am not representing, in the sense of interest to us, that I am communicating something important; I am representing where the water is. The complexity and lack of an agreed resolution of the debate that Grice and others initiated is notorious, but we should not lose sight of the fact that – somehow or other – we know the answer. When you agree to have a major operation, you bet your life on the surgeon having obtained good information about how things are from the sentences she or he reads in medical journals, hears from radiologists, reads in the referral note from your doctor, and so

---

[7] See Jackson (2006)

[8] Equally, it will carry *information* about the ambient temperature in one sense of "information." But think how you would feel if your doctor gave you your blood test results but refused to say whether or not they indicated that you were diabetic, saying "Those numbers regularly co-vary with whether or not a patient is diabetic, so I have given you the information you want." You would get angry, and that shows that you grasp the sense of "information" on which you have *not* been given the information you want. Our interest in these lectures is with that sense of "information."

[9] Grice (1989a, 1989b).

on. Somehow we latch onto the content in the intended sense; we latch onto the content in the sense of how things are being represented to be that is made available by coming across words and sentences in languages we understand.

Grice distinguishes the literal content of some sentence, on the one hand, from what is suggested, or implied in the everyday sense of "implied" (the implicatures, conversational or conventional, in his sense), on the other. It is, in these terms, the literal content that we are focusing on – the content we have called "ir-content," the way a sentence represents things to be in the intended sense of "representation" – and are insisting can be winnowed out from the various bits of information that come along with any assertoric production of a sentence. The distinction between the literal content of, say, "He has been sober all week" and what is implicated by producing it (that he is something of a drinker) is sometimes treated simply as a distinction to be defended at an intuitive level. I agree, with the majority, that the distinction is intuitively compelling – our students latch on very quickly to the idea that it is not part of the literal content of "He has been sober all week" that he's something of a drinker.[10] However, there is a more fundamental point to be made, one that, it seems to me, Grice would have agreed with.[11] The point is that there had *better be* such a distinction, and it had better be the case that we have a grasp of it. Otherwise sentences would not be the marvelously rich source of information that they manifestly are.

I hope these remarks explain why I have allowed myself to talk of *the* informational or representational content of sentences. And given that we may do this, surely we should think of such content as part of a sentence's meaning. For reasons we will canvass shortly, it would be a mistake to *identify* the meaning of a sentence with its ir-content, but its meaning determines its ir-content (assuming it is one of the sentences with ir-content, see below). That is, difference in ir-content implies difference in meaning but not conversely. Similarly, we should think of the contribution a word like "water" or "Plato" makes

---

[10]   For an affirmation that we should all accept the distinction, see Strawson (1990). See also Jackson (1987, ch. 5)

[11]   And one the later Wittgenstein would have disagreed with, going by Brandom's (2008, pp. 4–5) remarks, where he argues that Wittgenstein denies the existence of uses that "form a privileged center on the basis of which one can understand more peripheral ones."

to the ir-content of sentences like "There is water nearby" and "Plato was a great philosopher," respectively, as part of the word's meaning.

5. Why we need possible worlds

I have been talking freely of a sentence's ir-content. How should we model such content, how should we represent ir-content? The obvious way is by borrowing an apparatus familiar from possible worlds semantics. But then a natural thought is that the very moment we do this, we depart from commonsense and thereby from our aim of offering a folk theory. I will argue that this natural thought is mistaken but it will help to have the possible worlds account spelt out first.

The possible worlds account applies to a subset of sentences in English; the subset we have been implicitly restricting ourselves to all along, those that serve to represent how things are: sentences like "Snow is white," "Water is nearby," and Stanley's example, "Bill Clinton lived in Arkansas." The precise membership of this subset is controversial. Most agree that "Hooray" doesn't belong to it – exclamations express attitudes without representing them, or indeed anything – but it is controversial whether or not "If it rains, the match will be cancelled" and "Greed is good" belong to this subset. Maybe one or both of indicative conditionals and ethical sentences don't play the role of representing that things are thus and so. Noting this fact gives us one demonstration that questions of meaning outrun questions of ir-content. For we address the question of whether or not "If it rains, the match will be cancelled" or "Greed is good" represent that things are thus and so by asking about their meaning. This would be a nonsense operation if the very supposition that they have meaning implies that they have ir-content. (Thanks here to many, but David Plunkett especially).

We start with the simplest case, the case where there is no need to worry about centering. For sentences where we do not have to worry about centering, a sentence represents by making a partition in the space of possible worlds, a partition in logical space. For such a sentence, S, there is a function from S to a set of possible worlds. Each world in that set is a complete way things might be consistent with how the sentence represents things to be. Each world in this set is a complete way things might be in the sense that every "i" is dotted, every "t" is crossed. It is this feature that makes them count as possible *worlds*. In understanding S, we are able, in principle, to know which worlds are in this set and which are not. To know that some given world *w* is in the set, we don't, however, have to be able to discriminate *w* from any other world in thought (which is anyway impossible, for there are infinitely many possible worlds, whereas we are finite beings). Typically, we know that *w* is in the set in the sense that we know that any world that is thus and so is in the set, where indefinitely many worlds fall under "thus and so," and we know that *w* is thus and so. The putative information provided by asserting S is that we inhabit a world in that set. Thus a sentence's ir-content is this set of worlds. This set is not the same as S's meaning in the everyday sense of meaning (as we have noted, but more on this shortly). Finally, S is true if and only if its ir-content contains the actual world.

I said earlier that we could *stipulate* that understanding S is knowing which worlds are as S represents things to be, are the putative information provided by S (in the sense that we are being told that our world is one of them). This comes to stipulating that in order to understand S, one must know which worlds are in S's ir-content. We noted that this would not be in accord with our ordinary usage of "understanding," citing cases of what we might call imperfect or incomplete understanding. Moreover, there are cases where what seems to be the case is that someone understands a sentence in the sense of being able to know *in principle* which worlds are in a sentence's ir-content, without what is in principle possible for them being in fact the case. Take the pair of sentences: "There are wives" and "There are husbands." We should, I think, allow that someone might understand both sentences while failing to realize that they have the same ir-content, that the worlds at which the two sentences are true are one and the same. Although that person could in principle come to realize the identity in content – by which I mean that they do not need to carry out an experiment to make the discovery, reflection on their grasp of the meanings of the sentences and the words in them is enough – they may not do so in practice.

These remarks prompt two questions. First, why should we allow that they understand the sentences *before* they work out that they are true at the very same worlds? Well, *how* were they able to work out that the two sentences are true at the very same worlds? Didn't they have to use their understanding of the sentences and the words in them, in which case they must have, in some good sense, understood the sentences before realizing that they are true at the very same worlds? Secondly, why hold that the worlds in which things are as the two sentences represent them to be are the very same worlds? Why not work with a more fine-grained account of worlds? Well, if we gave God the task of making a world as "There are wives" represents things to be, the task would be one and the same as giving God the task of making a world as "There are husbands" represents them to be. I cannot see how one might differentiate one task from the other, anymore than one could distinguish being the shape of an equiangular triangle from being the shape of an equilateral triangle. In the second case there is just the *one* shape, differently represented; in the first, there is just *one* way for a world to be, differently represented. Similar remarks apply to pairs like: "Some glasses are half-full" and "Some glasses are half-empty," and "Some lions are dangerous" and "Some dangerous things are lions" (I give the second example to illustrate that identity in ir-content is compatible with difference in conversational implicature).

What is going on? Plausibly, we have a processing issue. Grasping the content of structured representations involves a certain amount of thought. Switching between Arabic and Roman numbering systems is an example we are all familiar with. I may (do) understand *CCXLVIII* in the sense that I know the significance of each symbol and of the way the symbols are arranged, and I could in principle work out the number it names and give that number in the Arabic system. But it isn't a totally elementary task and the process is a fallible one. The processing issue becomes especially salient in the case of very long, complex sentences. I might know how each of S_1, S_2, S_3, etc. represents things to be, and I know the effect of conjoining and disjoining sentences on how things are being represented to be. In this sense, but only in this sense, I know in principle how some horrendous disjunction of conjunctions made from S_1, S_2, S_3, etc. represents things to be. In practice, however, I may have no hope of recovering the content.

The remarks of the previous few paragraphs have been something of a digression. They remind us that understanding cannot simply be identified with grasping content in the ordinary sense of understanding, and also that meaning and ir-content are not the same.[12] The members of the pairs given above differ in meaning while agreeing in content. However, what is crucial for these lectures is the core claim that very often understanding delivers knowledge of how things are being represented to be. That is why we want to understand a word like "benign," and how combining words in various ways can produces sentences that represent, and are known to represent, that things are thus and so.

Why did we give *S*'s representational content in terms of a set of *worlds* in the sense explained above – every "t" is crossed and every "i" is dotted? Why appeal to an infinite set when we have recently acknowledged that our finite minds cannot distinguish an infinite set of possibilities? One reason is that it does no harm to include too much, whereas including too little would rob us of informational capacity. But the main reason is that we have to respect the point that a sentence, and likewise plans and maps, leave many things open. "It's benign" leaves open where the tumor is located; a house plan typically leaves open where the dog kennel is to be; and of course neither will have anything to say about whether the Higgs Boson exists. In representing ir-content, we have to capture *both* what is represented and what is *not* represented. We can think of that which unites the set of worlds in *S*'s content as giving how *S* represents things to be, with the matters on which the sentence is silent being the points of variation across the set. The set for "Some things are round" is the set of worlds containing at least one round thing, but that will be the sole point of similarity common to the set. If an all-powerful god were set the task of making a world which is as "Some things are round" represents things to be, she would complete her task once she had made a world with one round thing. But such a world would *ipso facto* represent a great deal more. This is why if she had to capture the ir-content, she would need to make infinitely many worlds, differing in all the ways consistent with the existence of at least one round thing – or better, as arguably not even a god can make infinitely many worlds, she would have to make an awful lot of worlds and then say something like "and so on and so forth."

---

[12] In later lectures we will note more reasons for distinguishing ir-content from meaning.

It is time to address the question, In appealing to possible worlds, am I departing from the realm of folk theory? There are two quite distinct issues on the table here. One is an issue in analytic ontology; the other is an issue about how we should think of information in these discussions. I will address the second issue first.

Here is the quote from Stanley (2007, p. 5) given in Lecture One, now with emphasis added:

> Suppose that Hannah utters ... "Bill Clinton lived in Arkansas" ... Hannah imparts certain information *about the world*.

I think he is right to talk of information in terms of worlds. We need to think of information in terms of categorizing worlds. As Stanley says, the information is *about the world*. Many, and I think (*think*) this is Stanley's position despite the word "world" in the quotation, think of information in terms of relations to propositions in a sense of proposition other than the set of possible worlds one. But consider someone who goes to a lecture on global warming and leaves the lecture remarking on how much they have learnt in terms of new propositions to assent to but wondering what, if anything, they have learnt about the kind of world we live in. They have seriously misunderstood the whole point of the lecture. Information about global warming, or the structure of space–time, or where the treasure is, or the best place for coffee, *is* information about the nature of the world we inhabit. It follows that we have to think in terms of categorizing worlds into those that are as the information has it and those that are not; that is to say, putative information is ir-content, where that content is a set of worlds that fall into the relevant category (or the set of centered worlds, but we are suppressing that complication for now).

Why hasn't this point been more widely granted? I think the reason is that talk of information and putative information naturally suggests belief, and we know that sets of worlds individuate belief contents too coarsely. The belief that there are wives is distinct from the belief that there are husbands, for it is possible to believe that there are wives without believing that there are husbands, and conversely. When you have one belief without the other, you are making an *a priori* detectable mistake, but that's possible. To say otherwise would be wrongly to identify what is *a priori* the case with what is infallibly believed. All the same, belief is a world-directed state; it aims at getting the world right. When I believe that the housing market has not yet reached the bottom, I am taking our *world* to be a certain way, and my belief is true just if our world is one of the worlds where the market has not yet bottomed. The point that sets of worlds are too coarse-grained to be the contents of belief tells us that belief is more than an attitude to sets of worlds; it doesn't tell us that belief isn't *at least* an attitude to sets of worlds.

6. Voyages through logical space

One of the most appealing features of the possible worlds way of thinking of information, understanding, and representation is the way it enables a compelling account of information transfer – communication, as we called it earlier – between users of a common language. Here is the account, set out step-wise.

> You come across a sentence that you understand.
> You have reason to trust it.
> Its ir-content is a set of worlds of the relevant kind.
> In understanding the sentence you know in principle what kind that is.
> You know that you and the token sentence are in the same world.
> You infer that you yourself are in a world of the relevant kind and you know what that kind is.

This is the 'voyages through logical space' picture of what happens when we acquire information through coming across sentences we understand and accept. We locate ourselves in the region of logical space where things are as the sentence represents things to be (unless we already locate ourselves in that region). Of course there is no movement through logical space in the sense of moving from one world to another. We are always and forever in just the one world, the actual world. What happens is that we change our view as to where in logical space the actual world (our world) is. Or at least that is what happens in the standard case where we come across sentences we trust, understand, and accept as correctly representing how things are.

Sometimes we move credences instead of changing in an absolute sense our view about where we are in logical space. If I accept what is said at a lecture arguing that global warming is a reality, I locate myself in the region of logical space where the worlds are ones where global warming is taking place, but if I am impressed but not fully convinced, I may move more credence into the region but refrain from definitively locating myself within it. And sometimes we neither locate ourselves among the worlds which are as some sentence we come across represents things to be, nor do we move credence into the region where things are as the sentence represents things to be. Our response to a sentence coming from the mouth of a known crackpot may be to locate ourselves anywhere but in one of the worlds where things are as he says they are, or it may be to move credence away from those worlds. But in this kind of case we are still using our grasp of the set of worlds which are as a sentence represents things to be, but are using our grasp in the interests of steering away from a region instead of steering toward it.

7. How to finesse the issue in analytic ontology

The issue in analytic ontology is, as we all know only too well, the status of the infinitely many possible worlds, only one of which is the actual world, that appear in the possible worlds account of information-cum-representation. Modal realists (extreme modal realists, to their opponents) hold that they are all, in a sense, variations on the actual world. Each point in logical space is of a kind with the actual world. The people in all the non-actual possible worlds are every bit as concrete as you and I, as the people in the actual world; and in the non-actual worlds where people and dogs are warm-blooded, their blood is warm in the same sense as that of the people and dogs in our world. Despite Lewis's powerful advocacy, few can bring themselves to believe this. Lewis called his vision a "philosophers' paradise" (1986, ch. 1), in order to highlight all the good things theoretically minded philosophers could do given an infinite stock of possible worlds of a kind with our world. However, most of us think of modal realism as an ontologist's nightmare. Having said this, I think it would be a serious mistake to require anyone appealing to possible worlds to first solve the problem in analytic ontology set us by possible worlds. It would be like asking those who use numbers to first solve the problem in analytic ontology set us by numbers. In order to make good sense of information and representation, we have to appeal to a set of possible worlds, a logical space. Or try to imagine doing probability theory without event spaces. Or – I might add – try to imagine doing philosophy of language or mind or ethics, or voting theory if it comes to that, minus reflections on possible but non-actual cases. Voting theory, for example, is replete with discussions of the effects of one or another voting system in one or another possible case, and these discussions are clearly crucial to sensible discussions of the strengths and weaknesses of the very many voting systems around – first past the post, preferential, optional preferential, proportional, etc. What is more, the folk are perfectly comfortable with the role of possible cases in discussions of voting systems – and chess openings, and tax policy, and where to go for their next holiday, and the best route into the city in peak hour, and the problem of evil, and so on.

I am not suggesting that philosophers should not worry about the question in analytic ontology. Of course we should. I am saying that we should not throw out the baby with the bath water. What is more, I think that, although we should reject Lewis's view that each point in logical space is a concrete world of a kind with the actual world, we need to think of each point as being, as we might say it, *conditionally* concrete. Each point represents what it would take for things to be as some sentence represents them to be, and what it would take is a complete, concrete way to be. What it *would take* for "There are only two electrons" to correctly represent how things are is every bit as concrete as our world. There is only one concrete possible world, *pace* Lewis. It is the actual world, the one we are in, and it contains more than two electrons. But for things to be as the sentence "There are only two electrons" represents them to be, there *would* have to be a *concrete* world with exactly two electrons.

We can put the key point in terms of the voyages through logical space picture given a little while back. In figure 2.1, the circle is the ir-content of sentence, *S*. The bold arrow represents the voyage that coming across *S* "invites" one to take through logical space, unless one already locates oneself inside the circle. The point we have just been making is that the invitation is *not* an invitation to locate oneself in an abstract entity, whatever that might come to. It is an

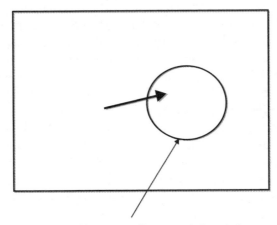

Worlds in which things are as S represents them to be

Figure 2.1

invitation to locate the one and only concrete world somewhere inside the circle.

8. The need for centered worlds

I now come to the complication set aside earlier. There is a simple and decisive reason why we cannot capture the ir-content of all sentences in terms of a set of worlds. Some sentences give information about parts of worlds in a way that cannot be reduced to information about worlds. These sentences are unlike, say, "Part of our world is hot," which gives information about part of our world but in a way that *can* be reduced to information about worlds: its ir-content is the set of worlds with a hot part.

There is substantial agreement these days about the phenomenon – sentences that give information that is *irreducibly* about parts of worlds – and the corresponding need for centered worlds.[13]

---

[13] For a sample of views against a background of broad agreement about the need for centered worlds or something like centered worlds, see, e.g., Perry (2001, esp. §6.2 and §8.1); Lewis (1979); Stalnaker (1999b; 2008, ch. 3). These discussions typically focus on the need in the case of certain thoughts; our concern is primarily with sentences.

When I utter "I have a beard," I am making a claim about how things are; I am providing information; I am representing. That is obvious. However, I am saying more than that the world I am in has at least one beard. It would be wrong to treat the ir-content of the sentence as the set of worlds containing at least one beard. I am saying that *I* have a beard. One might naturally respond that this means that the set of worlds that captures the content of "I have a beard," coming from my mouth, is the set of worlds where Frank Jackson has a beard. But that response treats my utterance of "I have a beard" as representing who it is who has the beard, namely, Frank Jackson. For, remember, the rule for matching content to sets of worlds is that what is being represented is that which is in common to the worlds in the content, and what is not being represented is that which varies as one runs through the worlds in the content, and a feature common to the set of worlds where Frank Jackson has a beard is that it is the very same person, Frank Jackson, who has the beard in each world. However, someone totally confused about who they are – someone waking from a coma suffering from serious amnesia, as it might be – may be in a position to utter "I have a beard" (perhaps he can feel the beard on his chin, as we noted in Lecture One). He knows that things are as he is representing them to be, while knowing that he does not know who he is. Is he perhaps representing that *someone or other* has a beard? No. Take our amnesiac. Perhaps he hasn't got around to feeling his chin yet but can see a face in a mirror on the wall and that the face has a beard. He is not sure whose face it is, as he cannot yet recognize his face.[14] *That's* the situation where it is right for him to utter "Someone or other has a beard," but that is *not* the situation he is in when he knows that he himself has a beard and utters "I have a beard."

It can be tempting to see an ambiguity in the point that, in saying "I have a beard," I am not saying who I am, the point that told us not to give the content with a set of worlds where some given person (be it me, you, or whoever) has a beard. You might say that there is a special property of I-ness, something each of us alone has. I have my I-ness, you have yours, she has hers, and so it goes on. The sense, then, in which I am not saying who I am is that I am not saying that it is the so and so who has (my) I-ness, for any and every value of so

[14] This is a variant on Perry's (1979) pants-on-fire case.

and so. To say who I am is to say who has my I-ness, and I am not doing that. On this view, the set of worlds that gets the content right can be specified as follows: the worlds where the so and so has my I-ness and the so and so has a beard, the worlds where the such and such has my I-ness and the such and such has a beard, the worlds where the thus and so has my I-ness and the thus and so has a beard, etc. In one sense, different people have a beard in different worlds in the content, for in some worlds it is the so and so who has the beard, and in others it is the such and such, etc. In another sense it is always the same person who has the beard, for it is always whoever has my I-ness who has the beard. On this way of looking at things, we are allowing an extra dimension of variation across possible worlds. As well as variation in the distribution of properties, we have variation in which individuals have those properties in a sense which does *not* supervene on the distribution of properties. Two worlds can be property instance for property instance alike, but in one I am (or you are) the so and so, and in the other I am (or you are) the such and such. We have an extra potential point of variation among worlds, something which some think of, or seem to think of, as a feature that outruns anything to be found in the world-view of science.

One way to object to this view is to highlight the mysterious nature of the posited additions. What do they cause? How might one detect them? How could reflections *per se* on the way certain sentences provide information or represent support such an exciting thesis in metaphysics? The simplest objection, however, is the argument from the outside observer.[15] Someone observing an utterance of "I have a beard" can say whether it is true or false merely by observing whether or not the person saying it has a beard. If they do, it is true, whereas if the person producing the sentence doesn't have a beard, it is false. Our observer does not have to carry out an investigation into whether or not the person making the utterance has the right I-ness, whatever precisely it would be to carry out such an investigation. But if how someone represents things to be when they say "I have a beard" is that the thing with their I-ness has a beard, where their I-ness may or may not be the I-ness of the producer of the sentence token, there would be extra work to do. And there isn't.

---

[15]   Jackson (2009a)

We seem to be in a jam. In saying that I have a beard I am saying more than that someone has a beard, but the attempt just surveyed to say what that more might be leads to serious trouble. The way out is to note that token representational structures, including ourselves and our sentences, often represent, carry information about, how things are, by representing how things are vis-à-vis themselves – the things doing the representing – in various ways. A barometer represents the air pressure in regions that stand in certain relations to it. A footprint represents how the foot that made it is. Now we draw on the key idea behind approaches to representation in terms of partitions of possibilities – what is being represented is what is in common to some set of possibilities – but think of the possibilities as centered worlds, worlds with one part designated as the center. When a token structure represents how things are at some point related thus and so to itself, the content is the set of centered worlds with things the way in question at that point, the point designated as the center. We replace worlds by centered worlds, and what unifies the set that gives the ir-content is that each center in its world is the appropriate way. For example, the ir-content of "I have a beard" is the set of centered worlds with bearded centers. This captures the point that what is being represented is that some particular thing has a beard. For what is in common to the set of centered worlds is that, in each, some particular thing – the center – has a beard. Equally, it captures the point that it isn't being represented which thing it is. For that which has the beard – the center – varies from one centered world to another. (However, the set of centered worlds with bearded centers is not the *informational value* of any given sentence token of "I have a beard" – to get that we need to combine the fact that the centers are bearded with the known relation between the centers and the token sentence. We will spell this out shortly.)

There are no potentially mysterious additions here. Centered worlds are no different from worlds. They aren't worlds with 'extras'. The only extra lies in our giving a part of a world, a perfectly ordinary part, a role in settling ir-content. When content is a set of centered worlds, what settles whether or not a centered world $<c, w>$ belongs to the content is how c is in w. That is, what determines whether or not a centered world is in the content is settled by how the part of that world designated as the center is in that world, but that part is a part of the world in the ordinary sense.

9. Getting information from sentences with centered content

I said earlier that one of the most appealing features of the possible worlds approach to ir-content is the compelling picture it gives of the transmission of information, of communication, using sentences we understand. The same is true for accounts of content in terms of sets of centered worlds, with a wrinkle to handle the small increase in complexity induced by centering.

When we get information through understanding sentences with centered content, a key part of the story concerns the way we get information *about the center* – the thing that is said to be thus and so. The information that one is in a world that belongs to a set of centered worlds with bearded centers is, *in itself*, no different from the information that one is in a world that belongs to a set of worlds with a beard somewhere or other. Absent information about the center, there is no difference in the informational value. But, of course, there is a big difference in the information one gets from "I have a beard" versus "Someone has a beard." The difference is all to do with information about the center. But this isn't a problem. For part of understanding the informational role of structures with centered content is knowing in principle how they are related to the centers in question. One who grasps the intended interpretation of a barometer's pointer reading knows that the reading represents the air pressure *where the barometer itself is*. One who grasps the intended interpretation of a petrol gauge's reading E knows that it is *the tank connected to the gauge* that is being said to be empty. One who understands "I have a beard" knows that the center in question is *the producer of the sentence*. Understanding representational structures with centered contents involves *two* things: knowing in principle the relevant set of centered worlds, and knowing how the token structures give information about the centers. To give a final example, familiar to all of us who get lost in shopping malls. Understanding the sentence "You are here," in a bubble with an arrow, on a map of a shopping mall, involves knowing in principle that its ir-content is the set of centered worlds with centers that stand in a certain relation to surrounding shops and walkways, and that the bubble's arrow tells you where the center is.

Here then is how transmission of information looks, spelt out for "I have a beard," much as we did earlier for sentences that do not have centered content. The additional complexity induced by centering is mild, as you will see

> You come across a token of "I have a beard."
> You have reason to trust it.
> Its ir-content is a set of centered worlds with bearded centers.
> In understanding the sentence you know in principle this ir-content.
> In understanding the sentence you know in principle that the center is the producer of the sentence.
> You know that you and the token sentence are in the same world.
> You know how you are related to the token sentence and thereby your relationship to the center in question.
> You infer that you yourself are in a world with a bearded center and how you stand with respect to that bearded center.

Here is how it looks in general:

> You come across a sentence token you understand.
> You have reason to trust it.
> Its ir-content is a set of centered worlds of the relevant kind (i.e. their centers are of the relevant kind).
> In understanding the sentence you know in principle what kind that is.
> In understanding the sentence you know in principle how the center is related to the token sentence.
> You know that you and the token sentence are in the same world.
> You know how you are related to the token sentence and thereby your relationship to the center in question.
> You infer that you yourself are in a world of the relevant kind, that is, its center is of the relevant kind, and how you stand with respect to that center.

Here it is again, using some jargon. The *ir-content* is the set of centered worlds. The token sentence is the *center locator*. The *informational value* is what you get by putting the first two together. Thus, for the sentence "I have a beard," the ir-content is the set of worlds with bearded centers, the center locator is the sentence token, and what you are in a position to learn, the informational value, is that the producer of the sentence token is bearded. Despite the jargon, what we end up with is simple and familiar enough to be called folk theory. The folk don't need to be told that a red flag has the content *danger*, that the flag's location says *where* the danger is, and that the informational value is that there is danger at that place. Of course, the informational value is not the same as the information someone who understands the sentence – or the flag – *takes away* from coming across the sentence or the flag. What you take away from coming across an assertion of "I have a beard" is in part a function of what you know about your relationship to the token sentence. Likewise, the information you take away from seeing the flag depends on your knowledge of how you are related to the flag. If it is off to the left, that's where the danger is; if the flag is right in front of you, that's where the danger is; and so on. The information you take away from coming across an assertion of "I have a beard" comes from the informational value of the sentence token plus information about how you stand to it, and will itself be centered information. It will concern where and when there is a bearded person vis-à-vis where you are yourself.

10. Saying things anew now that centering is in the story

We spoke at the beginning of this lecture of the connection between understanding a sentence and grasping in principle how things have to be in order to be as the sentence represents them. We cashed the latter out in terms of a set of worlds, those where things are as the sentence represents them to be: its ir-content. This needs revision once we acknowledge sentences with centered content. For these sentences, giving their content in terms of a set of worlds is mistaken in principle. It follows that giving their content in terms of a set of worlds where they are true is mistaken in principle. This matters, for centering is all over the place, as you would expect. Physical structures – and we and our sentences are physical structures – typically carry information about how things are vis-à-vis themselves in one way or another: the putative information is centered information. This point means, as we say above, that understanding which delivers information needs to be linked to in principle grasp of ir-content, plus in principle grasp of how token sentences give information about centers. The way sentences with centered content make available such a rich body of information about how things are is via our grasp of the centered worlds which are as the sentences represent things to be, plus our grasp of how the token sentences inform us about the centers: informational value comes from ir-content plus center location.

The point that ir-content is often not a set of worlds also has an important implication for a current controversy. Two-dimensionalism is unpopular in some circles (see, e.g., Soames 2005). However, one core claim made by two-dimensionalism is simply the contention that we need to acknowledge more than one content, and it can hardly be denied that one legitimate notion of content is the set of worlds at which a sentence is true (unless one rejects holus-bolus the worlds' way of thinking). It follows that the phenomenon of centering tells us that we had better be two-dimensionalists to some large extent. There is, that is, an important notion of content distinct from the set of worlds at which a sentence is true. I emphasize the word "impor-tant" in the previous sentence. There is a sense in which almost everyone grants that there is more than one content for many sen-tences. For almost everyone grants that, for many kinds of sentences, there are illuminating two-dimensional matrices[16] that map the dependence of truth on context for those sentences, that map, as it might be, "I have beard" into truth at x at t just when x has a beard at t. The disagreement of substance is between the two-dimensional-ists and those who insist that the *important* notion of content is the set of worlds at which a sentence is true. But if ir-content in general isn't the set of worlds at which a sentence is true, this cannot be right. For ir-content is important.

11. Where to now?

We have seen that, for certain first-person pronoun sentences, the set of worlds where they are true cannot be their ir-content. Similar points can be made about sentences with second- and third-person pronouns, like "You have a beard" and "She is singing." The point is obvious so I will simply sketch it for the second sentence. When I hear someone singing and can tell that it is a woman but have no

---

[16] As in Stalnaker (1999a).

idea who it is, I am entitled to use "She is singing" to say how things are. But there will be some specific person who is singing, Jane Doe let us say, so the worlds where the sentence is true will be those where Jane Doe is singing. But I am not entitled to represent my world as belonging to that set of worlds. It follows that the ir-content of my utterance is not the set of worlds where the sentence uttered is true.

What is perhaps not so obvious is that it is also true that the ir-content of sentences containing proper names, natural kind terms, and certain demonstrative adjectives cannot be identified with the worlds at which they are true. Arguing this is the business of the next lecture.

Lecture Three

Ir-content and the Set of Worlds Where a Sentence is True

1. Preamble

What does (an assertion of) "There are some round things" say about how things are, what putative information does it give? That there are some rounds things – obviously. How does a world have to be to be as that sentence says things are? It needs to contain some round things. At which worlds is the sentence true? At the worlds containing some round things. The ir-content of "Some things are round" is, it follows, the set of worlds where the sentence is true. However, for many sentences with ir-content, the set of worlds where the sentence is true is not their ir-content. As we have argued already, for sentences like "I have a beard" and "She is singing," we need sets of centered worlds, not sets of worlds. Ergo, sets of *worlds* where the sentences are true cannot be their ir-content. In this lecture we will look at more sentences for which it is true that the set of worlds where they are true is not their ir-content. However, for these sentences the crucial point is not that we need centered worlds to capture their ir-content (though often we do), but the way the rigidity of certain words in them means that the worlds at which the sentences are true cannot be their ir-content.[1]

We will look at four kinds of sentence: those containing proper names, those containing "actually" or "actual" working as

---

[1] Technically, rigidity can be seen as a special case of centering, one where the actual world is the center. However it isn't centering in the intuitive sense, the sense where the key point is that some sentences are irreducibly about parts (proper parts) of a world.

rigidification devices, those containing demonstrative adjectives, and sentences containing natural kind terms. For each, I will argue that the set of worlds where they are true cannot be their ir-content.

One might well ask, How can that be? Aren't the worlds at which S is true nothing other than those where things are as S represents things to be? This is why

(T)   "Snow is white" is true if and only if snow is white,

is an *a priori* truth. The left-hand side of (T) is true just if things are as "Snow is white" represents them to be, and one good way to give that way is to use the sentence itself, which is what is done on the right-hand side of (T). But then, it seems, S's ir-content must be the set of worlds where S is true. I grant that this line of argument can be seductive and I hypothesize that its appeal may explain why some have been reluctant to grant what seems to me the overwhelming case, taken in its totality, against the view that ir-content is always one and the same as the set of worlds where a sentence is true. In §5 below, and at more length in Lecture Five, I will explain where the seductive line of argument goes wrong. We will see how granting (T) – as of course we should – does not imply that the ir-content of a sentence is the set of worlds where it is true.[2]

2. The case of proper names

Questions about credence and questions about ir-content go hand in hand. I may give more or less credence to the information a sentence putatively provides, to things being as it represents them to be. And when I give credence to the information putatively provided by a sentence, I don't give credence to the sentence as such but to things being as the sentence represents them to be. The reason why my giving high credence to "There is a tiger nearby" makes me

---

[2]   But let me highlight that I have deliberately not talked in terms of truth conditions hereabouts. The set of worlds where a sentence is true might be thought of as its truth conditions, but equally the set of worlds, or the set of centered worlds, whose *actuality* is consistent with the sentence's truth might be thought of as its truth conditions. We discuss the difference between the two in Lecture Five, with a brief mention at §5 below. (Thanks here to Angela Mendelovici and Richard Chappell.)

jumpy lies in the high credence I give to things being as the sentence represents them to be. I, so to speak, see through the sentence to how it says things are. However, taking the ir-content of sentences containing proper names to be the set of worlds where the sentences are true gives manifestly wrong answers for the credence of those sentences.

Here is a case.[3] John Doe knows a bit about American literature but not much. He opens a book that has on its title page: "*The Adventures of Huckleberry Finn* by MARK TWAIN." In consequence, he gives the sentence "Mark Twain is the author of *The Adventures of Huckleberry Finn*" a very high credence. This is the right thing for him to do. He knows that title pages rarely 'lie'. Let's say he gives the sentence a credence of 99.5 percent. John Doe also knows that it is fairly unusual for one person to have two names and, what is more, that the probability of the conjunction of this person having a second name with that name's being "Samuel Clemens" is minute. He, therefore, gives the sentence "Samuel Clemens is the author of *The Adventures of Huckleberry Finn*" a credence of 0.01 percent. But the credence he gives each sentence is the credence he gives to things being as each sentence says they are. It follows that the two sentences do not have the same ir-content. They are, however, true at the very same possible worlds.

Suppose one said, heroically it seems to me, that contrary to appearances the two sentences have the same credence. John Doe is wrong. Which credence is the right one? 99.5 percent or 0.01 percent? There is no non-arbitrary way to jump, and averaging the two figures would seem, if anything, an even worse idea.[4]

In discussion, some have said that what we have here is one and the same proposition under two different modes of presentation. Fine, but that claim only addresses the problem if combined with the concession that credence attaches not to the proposition as such, but to it under one or the other mode of presentation. The two modes of presentation correspond to two different bearers of credence – otherwise we would be in Leibniz law trouble – and if there are two different bearers of credence, the bearer of credence for each sentence is not the set of worlds where the sentence is true. For that set is

---

[3] For other cases tackled in the same general spirit, see Chalmers (draft).

[4] Thanks here to discussion with David Braddon-Mitchell.

something our two sentences share. We get the conclusion I am after regardless.

The argument I have just offered turns on the fact that some things have two names. It belongs to a whole family of arguments, the most well known of which is perhaps the one that urges that the sentence "Hesperus = Phosphorus" has information value in a way in which "Hesperus = Hesperus" does not. How then, runs that well-known argument when framed in our terms, can their ir-content be one and the same, but that's what would be the case if we went for the worlds at which a sentence is true as their ir-content? Although I have put things in terms of credence – I think it makes the key point more vivid – and avoided using identity sentences as they can be controversial, the guiding thought is the same. The right credence to give "Hesperus = Phosphorus" differs in general from the right credence to give "Hesperus = Hesperus."

In any case, we can make trouble for the view that the ir-content of a sentence is the set of worlds where the sentence is true using cases in which the phenomenon of one thing having two names plays no role. We will now look at such a case. We start with some needed background.

Imagine that I am standing in front of a hotel with 26 internally identical rooms, named on their outsides *Alpha, Bravo, Charlie, ... , Zulu*. I am then drugged and placed, using a randomizing device, in one of the rooms while unconscious. I know this is going to happen. When I wake up I won't know which room I am in, and for each room the right credence to give to being in that room is 1/26.

This claim about credence seems to me self-evident, but I have met resistance so I should say something about the lines of resistance. Sometimes it is suggested that I'm assuming an outmoded, 'unduly qualitative' notion of a proposition. It is argued that one's evidence are the propositions one knows to be true, and although there is no qualitative proposition I know that favors my being in one room over any other – that follows from the fact that the rooms are qualitatively identical – there is a *demonstrative proposition* I know that favors one room over any other. When I wake I will know that I am in *this* room, pointing, as it might be, to the walls or floor of the room. Moreover, this piece of demonstrative knowledge favors my being in one room over any other, in that exactly one of the following conditionals is (necessarily) true:

If I am in this room, I am in Alpha.
If I am in this room, I am in Bravo.
...
If I am in this room, I am in Zulu.

This is correct but of no use to me. I have no way of knowing which conditional is the true one. Indeed, the question, Which conditional is true? is essentially the same question as, Which room am I in? We have reformulation, not discovery. This is no surprise. To borrow very freely from what may be Russell's most famous remark, philosophy of language is no substitute for honest geography.

Sometimes the resistance comes from a certain view about the individuation of perceptual experiences. Suppose I in fact wake up in *Bravo*. I am, runs the objection, wrongly assuming that my perceptual experience on waking up in *Bravo* is exactly the same (near enough) as my perceptual experience would have been had I woken up in *Charlie* or in *Zulu*. But, runs the resistance, we should individuate perceptual experience in part by its object. Perceptual experiences, or some perceptual experiences including the ones at issue here, are *object involving*. This means that my experience on waking in *Bravo* is quite different from that I would have had had I woken in one of the other rooms.

Here we need to distinguish the individuation issue from the epistemological issue. Maybe we should individuate perceptual experience in part by object; maybe we shouldn't.[5] But even if individuating by object is the right way to go, that is quite separate from whether individuating by object cuts any epistemological ice. Billiards is played (in Australia anyway) with one red and two white balls. The white or cue balls are exactly alike except that one has a small black spot. There is a small cost associated with putting the black dot on one white ball in each set of billiard balls. Would it make sense for the accountant of a factory that makes billiard balls to argue that, as perceptual experience is object involving, there is no need to bother with adding those black spots? I am sure we all agree that this would make no sense at all.

---

[5] For one discussion of this issue see Foster (2000, parts one and two). He favors the internalist view that we should not individuate by object perceived. My view, for what it is worth, is that we should individuate relative to the theoretical purpose at hand, and that most often means we should individuate the internalist way.

Now the situation I am in with respect to the 26 hotel rooms is like that we are all in with respect to logical space, except that in the case of logical space there are very many more than 26 possibilities we cannot discriminate between. As we said in the previous lecture, a world has every "t" crossed and every "i" dotted. By that standard, our knowledge of the world we are in is very meager. Relative to what we know, there are enormously many possible worlds that might credibly be the world we are in, might be, that is, the actual world. I am not talking here about *any* world consistent with what we know. I am talking about worlds consistent with what we know that have pretty much equal claim on our credence – worlds with roughly equal claim to be the one and only actual world.

This fact famously puts Lewis in a curious position. Because, according to him, each of these worlds is a concrete world, he has no marker, no distinguishing feature, to separate the actual world, the one we are in, from any of the others with roughly equal epistemic claim. He was well aware of this and bit the bullet. However, we – those who grant the key role of possible worlds in theorizing about information and representation but hold back from (extreme) modal realism – do have a marker. The actual world, our world, is the one and only concrete one: the one and only one with blood that *flows* and rocks that are *hard*, etc. This does not, though, alter the fact that there are indefinitely many worlds with equal claim to be the actual world. We, unlike Lewis, have our marker, but we don't know which out of a number of roughly equally credible candidate worlds possesses that marker.

We now have the background needed to see why the ir-contents of sentences of the form "N is F" are not given by the set of worlds where N, that very thing, is F.

Take the sentence "Kant is a great philosopher." We use this sentence to make a claim about how things are. It is one we all agree is true and has very high credence. (The probability that the great works attributed to Kant were in fact written by someone else is negligible.) It follows that if the set of worlds where Kant, that very person, is a great philosopher gives the ir-content of the sentence, the sum of the credences of those worlds must be very close to one. It isn't, that is the problem. We don't know Kant's, our Kant's, essential properties.[6]

---

[6]   See Lewis (1981) for the same point about Pierre's knowledge of London.

We know lots of properties of our Kant but these properties are common to many different people across logical space; they are, as we will put it, shared by all the *Kant-presenters*. In the hotel example, I faced 26 rooms, but there are indefinitely many Kant-presenters, for there are indefinitely many possible worlds that we give roughly equal credence to being the actual world, which contain someone distinct from our Kant but whom we cannot discriminate from our Kant. However, in the interests of keeping things simple, let us suppose that there are just 26 Kant-presenters. Call them $Kant_1$, $Kant_2$, ..., $Kant_{26}$. We are sure each is a great philosopher. We are sure one is our Kant but we do not know which one is our Kant. How then are we so sure our Kant is a great philosopher? Because we are all but certain that the following disjunction is true: $Kant_1$ is a great philosopher and our Kant = $Kant_1$, or $Kant_2$ is a great philosopher and our Kant = $Kant_2$, or ... $Kant_{26}$ is a great philosopher and our Kant = $Kant_{26}$. (If you didn't like the pretence that there are only 26 Kant-presenters, make this disjunction open ended.) And this disjunction of conjunctions entails that our Kant is a great philosopher. However, although we are all but certain the disjunction is true, each disjunct's probability is less than 1/26, or thereabouts; as the high probability of the disjunction is being shared across 26 roughly equally credible, mutually exclusive disjuncts. But the probability of the set of worlds where Kant, that very person, is a great philosopher is the probability of exactly one of those disjuncts. It follows that if the ir-content of "Kant is a great philosopher" was the set of worlds where Kant, that very person, is a great philosopher, what we say about how things are, the putative information we give out using the sentence, would be a piece of implausible speculation rather than the all but certain truth that it in fact is.

What we have just said can be captured in a diagram (see figure 3.1). The rectangle is logical space. The circle with the bold border is the region of logical space occupied by worlds where there is a Kant-presenter who is a great philosopher. The cigar shapes are the regions of logical space occupied by, in turn, worlds where $Kant_1$ is a great philosopher, $Kant_2$ is a great philosopher, ..., $Kant_{26}$ is a great philosopher. Nearly all our credence is shared among worlds inside the circle with the bold border. This means that there is very little credence flowing to the worlds inside each cigar shape. For each cigar shape takes up only a very small part of the region where nearly all

Figure 3.1

the credence is. But exactly one of these cigar shapes is the set of worlds where "Kant is a great philosopher" is true.

3. The difference principle

The argument I just gave in effect rested on a difference principle governing evidence deriving from causally induced signs. I am sure that it is no easy matter to state this principle in boilerplate fashion[7] but it is easy to illustrate. In the hotel example, the reason I neither knew nor had justified belief concerning which room I was in when I woke up is that I did not know of a relevant *difference* in the effect one room as opposed to any other would have on me. What I needed was a known difference and that I did not have. The reason we put the black dot on one of the cue balls in billiards is to ensure that there exists a known *difference* in what happens when a player looks at that cue ball rather than the other cue ball. The reason Hansel and Gretel laid down white pebbles when they were lead into the woods by their woodcutter father was to *differentiate* in a known way the path home. Paleontologists wonder whether the dinosaurs were

---

[7]   See Jackson and Pargetter (1985).

warm-blooded or cold-blooded. What makes the question hard is that it is unclear what *difference* it would make to the fossil record were they one rather than the other.

In terms of this difference principle we can give a simple, supervenience argument against the view that the ir-content of "Kant is a great philosopher" is the set of worlds where Kant, that very person, is a great philosopher. Our reason for holding that Kant is a great philosopher rests on an argument to the best explanation. Far and away the best causal explanation of what appears in various books, including especially but not exclusively ones with tokens of "Kant" in them, and in historical records etc. is that Kant is a great philosopher. These effects supervene on the distribution of properties. No difference in effects without a difference in the distribution of properties. It follows from the difference principle that our evidence for Kant's having been a great philosopher is evidence that someone who is thus and so was a great philosopher. But then it had better be the case that the ir-content of "Kant is a great philosopher" is such that it gets its great credence from what we are entitled to believe about the distribution of properties. But what we are entitled to believe about the distribution of properties is not enough to pick out Kant, that very person, across logical space.[8]

Does it matter that I didn't give a boilerplate version of the difference principle? It depends on the extent to which you are confident that the difference principle is essentially correct. I am sure it is. I cannot imagine a philosopher writing to paleontologists telling them that their concern to find the key difference in the fossil record that would allow them to decide, for some one or another dinosaur, whether it was cold blooded or warm blooded, rests on a confusion any more than I can imagine a philosopher arguing that billiard ball

---

[8] I am not saying that judgments of identity are *conclusions* of inferences from the distribution of properties. As we noted in Lecture One, often we recognize that some object is one and the same as one we have come across before. The conclusion picture is, if anything, even more implausible for cases where we track an object as it moves through space. No doubt, in some sense, our brains do some 'concluding' from information about the distribution of properties but it is at the sub-personal level. Moreover, if one were to make a model of how we represent and detect things to be when observing motion, it would be important to use *one* object, locating it at different places at different times – otherwise one would fail to capture part of what is represented and detected. However, and this is the key point, normally there is no one object with its essential properties, such that one would have to use it. (I am indebted here to discussion with Mark Johnston.)

makers should stop putting the black dots on one of the two cue balls. Some externalists have suggested to me that the fact that there is exactly one person, our Kant, who is the normal causal origin of our evidence for uttering "Kant is a great philosopher" warrants holding that the ir-content is the set of worlds where Kant, that very person, is a great philosopher.[9] But the dinosaur that is the normal causal origin of the part of the fossil record that tells us of its existence will either be warm blooded or cold blooded. That, in itself, cuts no epistemic ice.

4. The 'within a world' version of the argument using the difference principle

I made trouble for holding that the ir-content of sentences of the form "N is F" is given by the set of worlds where N, that very thing, is F, by noting certain limitations in what we know, or are entitled to believe, about our location in logical space. There is a more domestic version of the argument that operates inside a single world. I give it because I know that some find it easier to follow.

Suppose it turns out that our world is a world made up of 26 very widely separated, qualitatively identical space–time regions: R_1, R_2, ..., R_{26}. Perhaps the hypothesis serves to resolve all the extant problems in fundamental physics in such a striking and elegant way that it becomes as well supported as the kinetic theory of gases. This discovery would not mean that we could not name things, or that we could not make warranted, sometimes known to be true, claims about how things are, using sentences of the form "N is F." Mary Doe, for example, might name her son "John," and use, with justice given her knowledge of genetics, the sentence "John will grow up to look at least somewhat like his father" to make a claim about how things will be. The ir-content of this claim cannot, on pain of making her claim unjustified, be the set of worlds where John, that very person, grows up to look at least somewhat like his father. For she doesn't know, and doesn't have justified belief concerning, which region she and her John occupy. There are 26 people who might be

[9] This seems (*seems*) to be what Stalnaker (2008, p. 111) has in mind in his discussion of Lewis on Pierre.

her John and she cannot know, or have justified belief concerning, which one is her John.

This does *not* mean that she has to worry about the possibility that she has 26 sons.[10] For, corresponding to the 26 people who might be her son are 26 people who might be her. She can, we may suppose, be sure that each person who might be her has just the one son. That is how she can be sure that she has just the one son, while not knowing which of 26 possible sons in the actual world he is.

5. Sentences containing "actual" and "actually"

Our second example of sentences where the set of worlds where they are true does not give their ir-content are sentences with "actually" or "actual," working as rigidification devices.

By sentences with "actually" and "actual" working as rigidification devices, I mean sentences where those terms work as illustrated immediately below:

> "Actually *P*" is true at *w* if and only if "*P*" is true at the actual world.
> "The actual *F* is *G*" is true at *w* if and only if the *F* in the actual world is *G* in *w*.

And so on.

This is a piece of stipulation. The degree to which (ordinary) English has terms that work like this is a question for later. Obviously, English might have terms that work like this, but that does not mean that it in fact has terms that work like this. (The English spoken by some philosophers certainly has terms that work like this.)

What then do I, armed with my understanding of the rules for "actual" and "actually," as just explained, represent about how things are when I say "Actually some things are round"? The same as I represent about how things are when I say "Some things are round."[11] The reason is the combination of two facts: one is that it is trivial that I am in the actual world, and the other is that to take it that things are thus and so is to take it that the world *I am in* is

---

[10] Thanks here to discussion at the Jowett Society.
[11] Here I am agreeing with, e.g., Stanley (1997); see also Jackson (2004).

thus and so. It follows that, as vehicles for reporting how I take things to be, there is no difference between the two sentences. Each is right precisely to the extent that I take it I am in a world containing round things and wish to express the fact. It follows that the set of worlds right for capturing the ir-content of "Actually some things are round" is the very same set as the set for "Some things are round." But, as we noted at the beginning of this lecture, we know the right set for "There are some round things" and hence for "Some things are round": it is the set of worlds containing round things. It follows that the same set is the right set for "Actually some things are round." But this set is not the set of worlds where "Actually some things are round" is true. That set is the universal set, because "Actually some things are round" is true at w just if some things are round at the actual world, and some things *are* round at the actual world.

I emphasize that the reason for holding that the way "Actually some things are round" represents things to be is that we are in a world with some round things is not that it makes no representational odds in ordinary English whether we say "Actually P" or "P." It is true that it makes no representational odds, but the reason for this is that, in ordinary English, often "actually" (and the same goes for "in fact," "indeed," "really," etc.) works as a kind of emphasis provider that facilitates the transmission of information without changing the information up for transmission. In response to Harry's arguing that Fred Truman is the greatest post-war fast bowler England has produced, you might say "Actually Frank Tyson had a better strike rate." The role of the word "actually" is to make it clear that your assertion is made taking into account what Harry has just said. Again, if Harry says "The rate of inflation last year was 4.3 percent," and you think it was 3.4 percent and want to mark the fact that your confidence is sufficient to withstand the contrary evidence provided by Harry's assertion, you will say something like "In fact the rate of inflation last year was 3.4 percent." All this is by the way when asking if "Actually some things are round," *in the stipulated sense of* "actually," represents alike with "Some things are round." What is to the point is that to say how things are is to produce a sentence whose truth is consistent with some way things are being the actual way they are. This will be crucial when we address in later lectures (Lecture Five, especially) the question as to how it can be that the ir-content of some sentences differs from the worlds at which they are true.

Similar points apply to other types of sentences containing "actually" or "actual," in the stipulated sense of these terms. How "The actual prover of the first incompleteness theorem is identical to the prover of the second incompleteness theorem" represents things to be, the putative information it delivers, is not given by the worlds at which the sentence is true. Our sentence gives the information (in this case we can drop the "putative") that the prover of the two theorems is one and the same person. But the worlds at which the sentence is true include worlds where the two theorems are not proved by the same person. For instance, the sentence is true at a world w that meets the following specification: in w, the first theorem is proved by someone *other* than the person who proved it in the actual world (i.e. the prover isn't Gödel) but the second theorem is proved by the person who proved it in the actual world (i.e. Gödel). The reason our sentence represents that the two theorems were proved by the same person is that, given the stipulated way that "The actual F" works, the worlds that might be actual given the truth of the sentence are the worlds where the prover of the first theorem and the prover of the second theorem are one and the same person.

Our interest in these lectures is with how to understand the ir-content of ordinary language. Why have we just taken time to discuss the ir-content of an artificial language? The reason is that it is easy to see why, for these sentences, their ir-content is not the same as the worlds at which they are true. The set of worlds at which they are true is not the same as the set of worlds whose actuality is consistent with their being true. For each such sentence, the worlds at which the sentence is true differ from the worlds that might be actual given that the sentence is true. If ordinary English has words that work in the way the artificial language just described works, we will have a way of explaining how the ir-content of a sentence can differ from the worlds at which the sentence is true. More on this in Lecture Five.

6. Demonstrative adjectives

Our third example of sentences where the worlds where they are true do not give their ir-content are certain sentences containing demonstrative adjectives like "that person." (It will be obvious how the argument might run for other demonstrative constructions.)

I have (let us suppose) no idea who invented the zip, except that it was a man. But I know enough about zips to be able to assert with confidence "The inventor of the zip is one smart guy." In saying this I make a claim about how our world is that I am virtually certain is true. Now consider the inference:

Premise. The inventor of the zip is one smart guy.
Conclusion. The inventor of the zip, that very person, is one smart guy.

Is there anything risky about this inference? Of course not. You don't need extra information to assert the conclusion once you know the premise. Someone who asked about the investigation that justified drawing the conclusion from the premise would have the wrong end of the stick. Or suppose you and I are having a conversation about the person who proved the first and second incompleteness theorems in ignorance of who it was. In reflecting on the achievement, we might say "The person who proved the two theorems must have been a great logician," but we might equally say "The person who proved the two theorems, that very person, must have been a great logician." Are some extra enquires called for before saying the second? Of course not. Adding a demonstrative to a reference by properties or descriptions does not require extra information.[12]

However, the set of worlds at which "The inventor of the zip is one smart guy" is true is a very different set from the set at which "The inventor of the zip, that very person, is one smart guy" is true. What unites the first set is there being, in each world in the set, a unique inventor of the zip who is very smart in that world; what unites the second set is there being, in each world in the set, the person in the actual world who invented the zip, and their being very smart in that world. Moreover, the second set gets the information wrong. I do not know (we supposed) who invented the zip. This means the set of worlds that captures how I take things to be has to have different people inventing the zip in different worlds. The key point can be put this way. If the set of worlds where a sentence is true gives its ir-content, then by merely turning a reference by

---

[12]   I think (*think*) this is the kind of point Evans reports Grice as making in terms of not getting knowledge with a "stroke of the pen." See Evans (1982, p. 50).

description into a demonstrative reference, we would give information as to who it is who invented the zip.

Or suppose that you and I don't know who proved the two incompleteness theorems, though we know it was the same person. We are, all the same, in a position to affirm "The person who proved the two theorems must have been a great logician." And the worlds at which the sentence is true capture what we are entitled to believe about how things are. The worlds vary in who proves both theorems, which reflects what we don't know, while agreeing in having the prover in each world being a great logician, which reflects what we do know. However, the worlds at which "The person who proved the two theorems, that very person, must have been a great logician" is true don't vary in who proves both theorems. It is always the same person: the person demonstratively referred to by "that very person." But whenever we are entitled to affirm the first sentence, we are entitled to affirm the second sentence. Again, if ir-content is the worlds at which the sentence is true, we make the giving and gaining of information too easy. We don't know who proved the two theorems.

I emphasize that I am not saying that turning a reference by description into a demonstrative reference makes no difference to the meaning of the sentence. The change, for example, affects the behavior of the referential term under counterfactual suppositions in important ways that change meaning. What I am saying is that turning a reference by description in a sentence into a demonstrative reference isn't a wonderfully cheap way of giving or gaining information.

7. Natural kind terms

Our final example of sentences whose ir-content is not given by the worlds at which they are true are sentences containing natural kind terms. I will be unoriginal and focus on sentences containing the word "water."[13]

Historians of science tell us about the rise of modern chemistry and how it led to fundamental reappraisals of views about the kind of world we live in. They tell this story in many languages but we will focus on the story as it is told in English. A major part of this

---

[13] As I did in Jackson (2004)

story concerns the discovery of the molecular and atomic nature of many natural kinds and properties: ammonia is NH_3; gold has atomic number 79; water is H_2O; temperature in gases is mean molecular energy; and so on. When this story is told in English, those telling the story take it for granted that readers and hearers understand, for example, the words "water" and "H_2O" in such a way that they know the important discovery about our world that is reported by the words "Water = H_2O." But the worlds at which that sentence is true are the worlds at which water = water, and at which $H_2O = H_2O$. But it was no discovery that we are in a world where water = water, and $H_2O = H_2O$. Or consider the situation of people in 1750 before it was known that water = H_2O. They used sentences like "There is water nearby" to make claims about how things are. What they were saying about how things are can hardly be that there is H_2O nearby. They knew nothing of H_2O and maybe did not even have the concept. However, the worlds at which "There is water nearby" are one and the same as the worlds where there is H_2O nearby. It follows that we have another example where ir-content differs from the set of worlds where a sentence is true.

One response to this argument is that there is a crucial ambiguity in the contention that the worlds where "There is water nearby" and "There is H_2O nearby" are true are one and the same. The contention is true if you mean metaphysically possible worlds but false if you mean conceptually possible worlds. We will examine this suggestion in a bit of detail in the next lecture. For the rest of this lecture we will work on the widely, but far from universally, shared assumption that logical space means the space of the metaphysically possible, and that metaphysical possibility is the most inclusive notion of possibility. The alternative idea that we should think of the space of the metaphysically possible as a proper subset of the conceptually possible is set aside as business for the next lecture.

Another response to this argument is to urge that "water" is not a rigid designator. If this is right, the truth value of "There is water nearby" and of "There is H_2O nearby" differ at some possible worlds, and the worlds at which "Water = water" and "$H_2O = H_2O$" are true differ. We will examine this view about the word "water" in a little detail in Lecture Five, where we will suggest that the answer depends on *whose* usage of the word is in question. However, it is clear that some use "water" in a way that makes it rigid and the discussion to follow is premised on this (widely held) view about the word.[14]

However, the response I want to focus on is that the argument two paragraphs back fails to understand the significance of the environmental nature of content. According to this response, speakers in 1750 did *not* know what they were saying about how things are when they used "water," precisely because they did not know the key environmental fact that water is H_2O. But notice how implausible this claim is. It means that the philosophers around in 1750 should have warned English speakers that they do not know what they are saying when they use the word "water" in sentences like "There is water in the glass," perhaps adding as reassurance that scientists are working hard to find out what water is, and as soon as they have found the answer, we will know what we are saying when we use the word "water." Moreover, if English speakers didn't know what they were saying when they used the word "water," we might be led to ask if they knew what they were saying when they used the words "drought" or "thirsty." This doesn't seem very sensible. But of course the key point in response is that, *as we use the word "water" today*, we know perfectly well what discovery about what our world is like is reported by the sentence "Water = H_2O." If we didn't know, we would not have known the discovery historians of science are talking about when they say that Gay-Lussac and von Humboldt discovered that water is H_2O. But that discovery was neither that water = water, nor that H_2O = H_2O. On hearing the words "Water = H_2O," we moved our location in logical space – that's what it is to learn about the kind of world we occupy – but we already knew that we were located in worlds where water = water, and H_2O = H_2O. It follows that the ir-content of "Water = H_2O" is not the set of worlds where it is true.

Why would anyone take seriously the idea that people in 1750 did not know what they were saying when they used the word "water"? I think that a misreading of the importance of causation to reference may be at work. Consider the following passage, where Paul Bloomfield is summarizing "the persuasive moves that Kripke ... and Putnam ... used to explain how 'water' got its meaning":

---

[14] What is widely held is that "water" is rigid. Whether it is a rigidified description is another and more controversial matter.

A two sentence summary of the familiar story is that there was an intention of a linguistic community to refer to water, the physical material that turned out to be H_2O, with the word "water." Thus, it was H_2O that causally mediated the *use of the word "water"* even before we discovered that water is identical to H_2O. (2001, p. 120; my emphasis)

I choose this passage precisely because it is presented as a report of conventional wisdom.

Bloomfield is reporting a picture on which certain causal facts determine the meaning of the word "water" in the sense of how we use the word. No puzzle, it might then be said, about how it could be that people in 1750 did not know what they were saying when they used the word "water." They did not know the relevant causal facts and they did not know that water is H_2O. I do not know if Bloomfield would draw this conclusion, but I think some have (they tell me they have at conferences).

There are two reasons for not drawing this conclusion. First, any causal connection that uses of the word "water" have to H_2O, they have to the kind that fills the oceans and rivers, and falls from the sky and is, in many manifestations, potable, odorless, and liquid. That follows from Leibniz's law. H_2O *is* the kind that fills the oceans and rivers, and falls from the sky and is, in many manifestations, potable, odorless, and liquid. There is no mediation done by the one that is not done by the other, for there is no 'other'.[15] Secondly, we are not forced to use words in one way rather than another. The plausible view about how people used the word "water" in 1750 is that they used it to tell about the kind that fills the oceans and rivers, and falls from the sky and is, in many manifestations, potable, odorless, and liquid. That is what they knew about, and, for obvious reasons, we typically use words to tell about what we know about. Of course, I am agreeing that there is *something* that was unknown in 1750. People did not know the set of worlds at which "There is water nearby," e.g., is true. For they did not know that this set was

---

[15]   A complication. Strictly, it is water molecules that are identical to H_2O molecules. But this does not alter the fact that the causal transactions mediated by aggregations of H_2O molecules are one and the same as those mediated by the kind that falls from the sky and all that. (It is sometimes observed that the chemistry of water is tricky in ways that matter for some claims philosophers make. Fair enough, but the key points about language can be made using, e.g., the tigers-smigers example instead. Everything I say here could be recast in terms of that example.)

the set of worlds where "There is H_2O nearby" is true. That indeed is why I think the ir-content of "There is water nearby" is not given by the set of worlds where the sentence is true.

I am not, I emphasize, suggesting that there isn't a puzzle here that needs attention. If the plausible view is that people in 1750 used "water" to tell about the kind that fills the oceans and rivers, and falls from the sky and is, in many manifestations, potable, odorless, and liquid, how come "water" in our Earthian mouths doesn't refer to XYZ on Twin Earth, for XYZ is the kind on Twin Earth that fills the oceans and rivers, and falls from the sky and is, in many manifestations, potable, odorless, and liquid? We can all agree that that question needs serious attention. We address it in Lecture Five.

In arguing earlier that "Mark Twain is the author of *The Adventures of Huckleberry Finn*" and "Samuel Clemens is the author of *The Adventures of Huckleberry Finn*" differ in their ir-content, we noted that the two sentences can differ markedly in the credence we give them. A similar argument is available for "water" and "H_2O" sentences. As we said earlier, when we attach a credence to how a sentence says things are, we are not attaching it to the sentence *per se*. This means that if the ir-content of "There is water nearby" is one and the same as that of "There is H_2O nearby," the sentences must always have the same credence, including for those ignorant or in doubt about the identity of water with H_2O. This is very hard to believe. It is close to common ground that the identity of water with H_2O is *a posteriori*. If that is right, it is rational to give the sentence "Water = H_2O" a credence of less than one, but then it is rational to give, for instance, "There is water nearby" and "There is H_2O nearby" different credences.

8. A passing comment on centering

A sentence like "There is water nearby" is exactly the kind of sentence we would expect to have centered content. For it makes a claim about how things are in a part of a world, the part that is nearby, and typically the nearby in question will mean near to the person producing the sentence. When a guide in the Gobi desert sniffs the wind and says "There is water nearby," he is saying that there is water near to where he is. This means we will need centered worlds for the very same reasons we need them for "I have a beard," the reasons we canvassed in Lecture Two. An obvious question then is, Can we capture the sentence's ir-content with the set of centered worlds at which the sentence is true, the set of centered worlds with water near their centers? No. That set will be the set of centered worlds where H_2O is nearby, and "There is water nearby" does not, as we have seen, have the same ir-content as "There is H_2O nearby." The same goes for a sentence like "I read Kant," a sentence whose ir-content is given by a set of centered worlds. The reasons that told us that the ir-content of "Kant is a great philosopher" is not given by the set of worlds where Kant, that very person, is a great philosopher show that the ir-content of "I read Kant" is not given by the set of centered worlds whose centers read Kant, that very person. The problem with taking ir-content to be the set of worlds where a sentence is true, for the sentences we have been focusing on in this lecture, cuts across the need for, in many cases, sets of centered worlds to capture ir-content. Centering is not what is causing the trouble; rigidity is causing the trouble.

9. Where to from here?

This completes our survey of sentences whose ir-content differs from the worlds at which they are true. What are the implications?

Surely, one thing is clear. The set of worlds where a sentence is true is one legitimate notion of content, as we said at the end of Lecture Two. It follows that those sentences whose ir-content differs from the set of worlds where they are true have two contents. This is sometimes taken to be an ambiguity thesis. It is thought that to hold that "water" sentences have two contents is to hold that "water" is ambiguous.[16] However, as will become clear in later lectures, this isn't the case. Rather, as we will see, *the* meaning of "water" is such that "water" sentences have two contents (or, better, the meaning of "water" in the mouths of some), and *the* meaning of sentences containing proper names is such that they have two contents.

I know many feel strongly that any two-content view is wrong-headed. Sometimes the opposition goes back to a point we discussed

---

[16]   A recent example is Bloomfield (2001, p. 120*n*).

in the second lecture. The idea is that information is not an essential part of the story about meaning. To which, in a nutshell, our reply was that the information that knowing the meaning makes available is crucial. It is why we pay for lessons in Russian before we go to Russia.

Sometimes the idea is that there is one content that presents itself in different ways. Water, the stuff, may present itself *qua* the kind that fills the oceans and rivers and falls from the sky and is, in many manifestations, potable, odorless, and liquid; or it may present itself under its chemical formula guise as H_2O. But this view is a two-content view in all but name. The two guises do the work of two contents. This fact can be concealed by the way the "two-presentation" view is presented. We are told that we did not know what "water" stands for until we knew that water was H_2O, but we knew enough to use the word in communication. For we knew that the word stands for stuff that manifests itself in the "watery" way, and that was good enough for communication. But, runs the presentation, there was always just the one stuff the word stood for – the stuff that turned out to be H_2O – and so the one content. But this story is internally inconsistent. For, according to it, under what circumstances did we use the sentence "Water is nearby" to communicate how we took things to be, before we knew that water was H_2O? When we thought that the stuff that was watery (to borrow the now standard abbreviation for the kind that is typically potable, falls from the sky, and all that) was nearby is the proffered answer. But that is what it *is* for the sentence to have the ir-content that the watery stuff is nearby.

Finally, sometimes the idea is that talk of two contents is a confused way of talking of one content's being a function of context. This seems to be what Stalnaker has in mind when he talks of "the metasemantic paradigm" (2003a, p. 208f.). Thus, to take the example discussed in the first lecture, the suggestion is that the content of "I have a beard" is a function of who says it, and the rule is: said by x its content is that x has a beard (I set aside the complications posed by time in the interests of keeping things simple). How then do you get the right answer for the information provided by an assertion of "I have a beard"? You get it from your knowledge of the way the (single) content is a function of who says it. Thus, might run the suggestion of the one-content theorist, the information provided by the sentence is that the producer of the sentence has a beard. I reply that this *is* a two-content theory, a two-content theory with an account of how the second content is delivered by the dependence of the first content on context. My only reservation about it is that the account leaves out the center location role of the token of "I" in delivering what we called informational value in Lecture Two, §8.

I think there is only one way to resist the case for a two-content view of the kinds of sentences we have discussed in this lecture: it is to repudiate the whole way of thinking that lies behind approaching ir-content in terms of divisions among possibilities, be they possible worlds or centered possible worlds. This is tantamount to rejecting the informational-representational approach to language, or at least to the parts of language we are focusing on – the parts, as we have put it, that serve the function of saying how things are; the parts that take us on voyages through logical space. I won't repeat what I have said already in defense of that approach to language. For the reasons I have given, this approach is, from my perspective, all but axiomatic.

There are, however, two quite different ways of being a two-content theorist. One way is to see the two contents as regions of *different* logical spaces; the other is to see the two contents as marking out different regions of the *one* logical space. The decision between the two is the main topic of the next lecture.

Lecture Four

Two Spaceism

1. One spaceism versus two spaceism: setting the scene

We need possible worlds to capture the fact that the information provided by words and sentences is about the world, to capture the representational nature of language, or, more precisely, of the parts of language we are concerned with. In the previous lecture I argued that the worlds at which a sentence is true are not always the ones that give a sentence's ir-content. For some sentences we need a second set of worlds – or centered worlds, given what we said in the second lecture. There are two places where we might look for the second set. We might work within a single logical space and seek a second set of possible worlds, or of centered possible worlds, within that space, to be the ir-content of those sentences whose ir-content is not given by the worlds, or centered worlds, at which the sentence is true. This is the 'two regions within one space' approach, or *one spaceism*.

The alternative is to multiply logical spaces. This approach is inspired by the response many have to the distinction Kripke, most especially, made us sensitive to: the distinction between what is meta-physically necessary and what is conceptually necessary – where the necessary *a posteriori* is thought of as metaphysically necessary but not conceptually necessary – and the correlative distinction between what is metaphysically possible and what is conceptually possible. The response (not Kripke's if I understand him aright) is to argue that we need two logical spaces. The most inclusive is the space of what is conceptually possible, and it has as a proper subset the space of what is metaphysically possible. The conceptually necessary is then what is true at every conceptually possible world; the conceptually possible is what is true at some conceptually possible world; whereas the metaphysically necessary is what is true at every metaphysically possible world and the metaphysically possible is what is true at some metaphysically possible world. To illustrate: suppose with the majority that "Any water is H_2O" is a necessary *a posteriori* truth, then it is true at every metaphysically possible world, but it is not true at every conceptually possible world. There are, on this two-space way of looking at matters, conceptually possible worlds where water is not H_2O.

2. Two spaceism and ir-content

Suppose this second way of looking at things is on the right lines. In that case I fudged a crucial question in the previous lecture. When I argued that, for some sentences, their ir-content is not the set of worlds where they are true, was I talking about the set of conceptually possible worlds or the set of metaphysically possible worlds? This can make all the difference in the world. I argued, for instance, that "There is water nearby" and "There is H_2O nearby" differ in their ir-content, while being true at the same possible worlds. But the latter is only true for metaphysically possible worlds would be the idea. For on the approach under discussion, there are conceptually possible worlds where there is water nearby but no H_2O nearby, and conversely. Again, I argued that "Water = H_2O" differs in its ir-content from "Water = water," while being true at the same possible worlds. That claim would only be true for metaphysically possible worlds. In similar vein, we would explain the difference between the way "Mark Twain is the author of *The Adventures of Huckleberry Finn*" represents things to be from the way "Samuel Clemens is the author of *The Adventures of Huckleberry Finn*" represents things to be, by noting that there are conceptually possible worlds where Mark Twain $\neq$ Samuel Clemens. And the explanation of how John Doe might correctly give the first sentence very high credence and the second sentence very low credence would lie in his giving very high credence to the conceptually possible (but metaphysically impossible) worlds where Mark Twain $\neq$ Samuel Clemens.

These reflections might naturally suggest that the space of conceptually possible worlds is the right space to represent representation and information, the right place to find ir-content. We can, is the suggestion, stay with the thought that ir-content is the set of worlds where a sentence is true, provided we insist that the set is the set of conceptually possible worlds and not the set of metaphysically possible worlds. What about the many cases that call for centered content? They would be handled in terms of sets of centered, conceptually possible worlds.

Crucial to the suggestion just bruited is the two-spaceist way of thinking about the necessary *a posteriori*, and the distinction between the necessary *a posteriori* and the necessary *a priori*. It is common ground (near enough by the standards of the community of philosophers) that there are necessary *a posteriori* true sentences, and close to common ground that "Any water is H$_2$O" is an example.[1] Also, it is common ground that "Any water is water" is an example of a necessary *a priori* sentence. There is, that is, widespread agreement that, at the level of sentences, there is a distinction between what is necessarily true *a posteriori* and what is necessarily true *a priori*. What is much more controversial is the two-space way of thinking about this distinction among sentences. I, following others, including Tichý and Stalnaker, have always taken the view that two spaceism *about possibilities* is the wrong way to think about the necessary *a posteriori* – necessary *a priori* distinction among sentences. There is an important distinction for sentences but it does not correspond to a correlative distinction among possibilities. Here is Stalnaker's way of putting the point: "[The view] we can all agree is wrong ... [is] that metaphysical necessity is a restricted kind of necessity" (2003a, p. 202).[2]

However, others take exactly the opposite view, and, despite the "we can all agree" in the quote from Stalnaker, describe the two-space position as the default, natural, or standard one. Here is a quote from Soames: "In my view, the natural, default position is that, of course, there are metaphysically impossible but epistemically possible world-states – ways the world could not genuinely be which we cannot know apriori that it isn't" (2005b, p. 199). And here is a quote from Lycan: "Consider the standard picture of logical space,

---

[1] More precisely, what is close to common ground is that the sentence is an example for those who use the word "water" rigidly, something we are all free to do and something some of us do. What we are assuming in this lecture and the previous one is that this is how we all in fact use the word. As noted in the previous lecture, alternative usages are discussed in Lecture Five.

[2] For Tichý's views, see Tichý (1983).

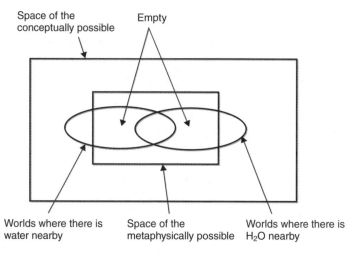

Figure 4.1

featuring ever-larger concentric circles. We can start with the usual three grades of possibility, nomic, metaphysical, and conceptual; the nomically possible worlds are a proper subset of the metaphysically possible, which in turn are a proper subset of the conceptually possible" (2009, p. 78).

We can use the picture Lycan describes as standard to diagram the way two spaceism would explain the difference in ir-content between, say, "There is water nearby" and "There is H_2O nearby." The outer rectangle in the diagram above would be the space of the conceptually possible, the rectangle inside it would be the space of the metaphysically possible. The two ellipses would be the ir-content of the two sentences, and, as indicated in figure 4.1, although the metaphysically possible worlds inside the two ellipses are the same, they differ in the conceptually possible worlds inside them.

The same diagram could be used to illustrate the way two spaceism would explain the difference in ir-content between "Mark Twain is the author of *The Adventures of Huckleberry Finn*" and "Samuel Clemens is the author of *The Adventures of Huckleberry Finn*." In both cases, the key point is that the 'track', the region outside the inner rectangle and inside the outer rectangle, is not empty. It contains conceptually possible but metaphysically impossible worlds where, for instance, water is not H_2O, and Mark Twain is not Samuel Clemens. Also, a diagram like this could be given for centered worlds. The ir-content of "I am near water" would differ from that of "I am near H_2O."[3] This would, presumably, be handled, on the two-space approach, by holding that although the set of metaphysically possible worlds with centers near water is identical to the set of metaphysically possible worlds with centers near H_2O, the set of conceptually possible centered worlds with centers near water differs from the set of conceptually possible centered worlds with centers near H_2O.

Despite Lycan's and Soames's urging that two spaceism is the standard or default way to go, and despite the way two spaceism seems to offer (as we have just been outlining) a simple way to distinguish the ir-content of "water" and "H_2O" sentences, "Mark Twain" and "Samuel Clemens" sentences, and so on, I remain unconvinced.

My arguments to come against two spaceism will be different from the one I made in Jackson (1998a). My argument there turned on a certain view about the classic examples of necessary *a posteriori* sentences, namely that the examples are the product of rigidification devices in natural languages. We do not need to invoke conceptual possibilities that are metaphysically impossible to explain the phenomenon. I stand by this argument[4] but I now think the two arguments I give below have the advantage of avoiding an issue which turned out to be more controversial than I had expected, and, more importantly, the arguments address more directly the key issues of information and representation that are on the table.[5]

However, first, a comment on terminology before arguing against the two-space position.

3. Which label: "epistemic" or "conceptual"?

Should we describe two spaceism as holding that the space of the *conceptually* possible has the space of the metaphysically possible as

---

[3] Of course, "There is water nearby" and "There is H_2O nearby" also call for centered worlds, because of the role of "nearby." I simplified earlier.

[4] For a recent defense see Jackson (forthcoming b).

[5] The main line of thought in what follows is a recasting and expansion of the argument in Jackson (forthcoming c). I am grateful to Oxford University Press for permission to use this material.

a proper subset, or as holding that the space of the *epistemically* possible has the space of the metaphysically possible as a proper subset?

I think there are two reasons in favor of using the "conceptual possibility" terminology, the terminology that Lycan, for example, uses in the quote given above. One is that what is epistemically possible is most naturally understood as what is possible consistent with what we know. But that would mean that water's failing to be H_2O is *not* epistemically possible, once we know that water is H_2O. However, the two-space idea is precisely that water's failing to be H_2O is possible in the more inclusive sense, independently of our knowledge that water is H_2O. Moreover, our knowledge that water is H_2O is perfectly consistent with the fact that our knowledge is not *a priori*, with the fact that water's not being H_2O is not something we can rule out *a priori*. This recommends thinking of the more inclusive sense of possibility as that which cannot be ruled out *a priori* – which is pretty much what Soames says – and "conceptually possible" would seem a good label for what is possible in this sense.

The second reason for avoiding the epistemic possibility way of talking is that it invites a way of thinking about the water–H_2O example that, whatever its intrinsic merits, is certainly not a variety of two spaceism. I mean the way of thinking that offers, as an explanation of the *appearance* of contingency attaching to water's not being H_2O, the fact that it *is* possible that there exists stuff that, while not being water (i.e. not being H_2O), is epistemically indistinguishable from water – it is a kind that is found in lakes and rivers and is typically liquid, potable, and colorless, etc. But this is not two spaceism. It is no part of this just given explanation that there is *any* sense at all in which it is possible that water might fail to be H_2O. What is being explained is an *illusory* appearance.

I now turn to the first argument against two spaceism.

4. Which possibilities, precisely, are the ones two spaceism holds are conceptually possible but metaphysically impossible?

Crucial to two spaceism is the view that there are possibilities in what I called above, the track: the region outside what is metaphysically possible but inside what is conceptually possible. What is more, these possibilities need to be right for explaining, for example, how "water" sentences can differ from "H_2O" sentences in how they represent things to be, and how "Mark Twain" sentences and "Samuel Clemens" sentences can have very different credences and ir-contents. There is no progress on the issue at hand in insisting that there are conceptual possibilities that are metaphysically impossible *unless* they do the needed job of separating out the ir-content of, for example, "Mark Twain is the author of *The Adventures of Huckleberry Finn*" from the ir-content of "Samuel Clemens is the author of *The Adventures of Huckleberry Finn*," and separating out the ir-content of "There is water nearby" from the ir-content of "There is H_2O nearby." This puts a constraint on the possibilities located in the track. They need to include possible worlds where water ≠ H_2O, and Mark Twain ≠ Samuel Clemens, where these possibilities are understood in a way that secures the needed difference in ir-contents. This, it seems to me, is where the trouble starts.

Take the proposal that there are conceptually possible worlds where Mark Twain ≠ Samuel Clemens first. Let w^* be one such world. In our world, w_a, which is of course both metaphysically and conceptually possible, Mark Twain = Samuel Clemens. Now how does Mark Twain in w_a stand to Mark Twain in w^*? The obvious answer is that 'they' are one and the same. And how does Samuel Clemens in w_a stand to Samuel Clemens in w^*? Consistency with the answer given for the same question asked of Mark Twain requires the answer that 'they' also are one and the same. But then, by the transitivity of identity, Samuel Clemens in w^* = Mark Twain in w^*. Exactly the wrong answer for the proposal under discussion. If it is to help with the question on the table, two spaceism must hold that Samuel Clemens in w^* ≠ Mark Twain in w^*.

The obvious, and as far as I can see only, way out is to deny that Mark Twain in w_a = Mark Twain in w^*, and likewise deny that Samuel Clemens in w_a = Samuel Clemens in w^*. The idea would be that there is no trans-world identity, or maybe that sometimes there is and sometimes there isn't, and this case is one of those where there isn't. The Mark Twain of w^* is not our Mark Twain; likewise the Samuel Clemens of w^* is not our Samuel Clemens. What we have is similarity of some substantial degree between our Mark Twain and w^*'s, and between our Samuel Clemens and w^*'s, enough to be counterparts in Lewis's terms.[6] However, by Leibniz's law, every similarity relation our Mark Twain stands in is one our Samuel Clemens stands in, and conversely. This means that the set of conceptually possible worlds at which "Mark Twain is the author of *The Adventures of Huckleberry Finn*" is true is one and the same as the set at which "Samuel Clemens is the author of *The Adventures of Huckleberry Finn*" is true *independently* of whether or not there is trans-world identity across the conceptually possible. This negates the whole point of going two space to start with. We are back where we were at the end of Lecture Three.

The only way two spacers can get "Mark Twain is the author of *The Adventures of Huckleberry Finn*" to differ in ir-content from "Samuel Clemens is the author of *The Adventures of Huckleberry Finn*" is by taking a leaf out of Lewis's counterpart theory and telling their story in terms of similarities *relativized to ways of referring.* Here is how it would look in outline: the ir-content of "Mark Twain is the author of *The Adventures of Huckleberry Finn*" is the set of conceptually possible worlds where someone like Mark Twain (our Twain, the one who is our Clemens) in the 'Mark Twain' way is the author of *The Adventures of Huckleberry Finn,* whereas the ir-content of "Samuel Clemens is the author of *The Adventures of Huckleberry Finn*" is the set of conceptually possible worlds where someone like Samuel Clemens (our Clemens, the one who is our Twain) in the 'Samuel Clemens' way is the author of *The Adventures of Huckleberry Finn.* But now the extra logical space is otiose. We can tell the story inside the one logical space. All we need is a reading of the relevant likenesses on which it is metaphysically possible to fall under one without falling under the other. What is metaphysically impossible is that Clemens and Twain, our Clemens and Twain, be distinct. There is nothing metaphysically impossible about there being two distinct persons, x and y, such that x is like that very person in one way, whereas y is like that very person in another way.

I have presented the problem for two spaceism in a "nothing is gained" form. But the malaise goes deeper than that, it seems to me. The identity of the possible worlds that are supposed to be conceptually possible but metaphysically impossible is deeply obscure.

---

[6]   Lewis (1968, 1986).

Take, to start with, the worlds alleged to be conceptually possible but metaphysically impossible where Mark Twain ≠ Samuel Clemens. What makes those possible worlds correctly described as ones where Mark Twain ≠ Samuel Clemens? Not the fact that they contain the Mark Twain and Samuel Clemens of our world, for in our world Mark Twain is one and the same person as Samuel Clemens, and two people cannot be one person. What is more, that's a conceptual impossibility. Another answer might be that these worlds contain someone who presents in the Mark Twain way (whatever precisely that way is, but presumably it will be to do with having properties that lead us to identify someone *as* Mark Twain) and someone who presents in the Samuel Clemens way (whatever precisely that way is, but presumably it will be to do with having properties that lead us to identify someone *as* Samuel Clemens) and these people are distinct in those worlds. That, however, is *metaphysically* possible. On neither way of spelling out what makes some worlds correctly described as ones where Mark Twain ≠ Samuel Clemens are those worlds conceptually possible while being metaphysically impossible.

Similar problems beset the idea of possible worlds which are conceptually possible while being metaphysically impossible, where water ≠ H_2O. What makes them worlds where it is *water* that fails to be H_2O? There would seem to be just two ways to go in answering this question. First, one might answer that what makes their water water is that both are H_2O. But H_2O's not being H_2O is conceptually impossible. That answer makes it *conceptually* impossible to have worlds where water ≠ H_2O. Second, one might answer that what makes their water water is its being a kind that fills the oceans and rivers, and falls from the sky and is, in many manifestations, potable, odorless, and liquid, or something on these lines (the details do not matter here). But H_2O's not being such a kind is *metaphysically* possible. The possible worlds where water ≠ H_2O that are supposed to be conceptually possible while being metaphysically impossible have vanished.

It might be thought that there is a third way to answer the question, What makes the water in the allegedly conceptually possible but metaphysically impossible worlds, where water ≠ H_2O, count as water? Say that the answer is its being water. Now this is certainly a third way to answer the question in the sense that different words are being used, but our question is not about words as such. It would, for instance, be misconceived to think that using French to answer the question might advance matters. Our question is about what unifies our water with the alleged water in the claimed worlds where water $\neq H_2O$, in a way that makes it right to describe the claimed worlds as ones where water $\neq H_2O$. And our argument is that neither of the only two answers with any appeal serves the needs of the two spacer. But suppose someone insisted that when they used the word "water" to answer our question, in the spirit of "and that's all the answer that is needed," what they had in mind was that what makes water water is its having some *sui generis* "water-making" feature. The trouble now is that there is no extra, *sui generis* property of being water. Someone who lists the properties of water, our water, starting with its being H_2O and including all the details about where and when it is potable, where it is to be found, how much of it is liquid, odorless, and colorless and all that, but thinks that, after doing all that, they must add to the list, on pain of leaving a key property out, that the stuff is water is confused. There is no further property, and, therefore, no further property to answer the "water-making" question.

It is, I trust, obvious that similar problems can be raised for the other examples given from time to time of possible worlds claimed to be conceptually possible but metaphysically impossible. All the same, let's quickly review one further alleged example that some find especially convincing.[7]

Many who hold that the constitution of an object is an essential property of it argue that some particular object's not being made of wood, in the case where it is in fact made of wood, is metaphysically impossible. Suppose they are right. Should we then say that a possible world where this very table – the one I am now writing on, which is made of wood – is not made of wood is an example of a world that is conceptually possible but metaphysically impossible? No. For what makes the table, in the claimed conceptually possible world where it is not made of wood, this very table? If a table's constitution is an essential property of it, part of the answer must be its being made of wood. But then the world said to be conceptually possible is no such thing. A table made of wood not being made of wood is conceptually impossible.

---

[7]   See, e.g., Soames (2005b, p. 198).

5. How working with the bigger canvass raises some of the same questions over again

I turn to the second problem for two spaceism. Let us grant the two-space picture in much the way outlined by Lycan. The most inclusive set of possible worlds is the set of conceptually possible worlds, with the set of metaphysically possible worlds as a proper subset (and the set of nomically possible worlds is a proper subset of the metaphysically possible ones, but they aren't in play here). What is more, the worlds that are right for representing information and representation are the conceptually possible worlds. We have been making trouble for an essential part of this supposition, the part that requires that there be worlds in what we called the track: the region outside what is metaphysically possible and inside what is conceptually possible. But let's now set that issue to one side. The problem I want to press below is independent of that issue.

The further problem arises from the fact that the logical space of the conceptually possible is being proposed as the right space for information and representation. On this view, the way language is able to give information about our world is to be understood in terms of how sentences and words carve up the logical space of the conceptually possible. What we learn when we hear "The big bang theory is true" is that we are in one of the conceptually possible worlds where there is a big bang. That is all well and good, and the basic framework is familiar from previous lectures, and we could introduce conceptually possible centered worlds as the need arose. But something else we can surely do with language is to pick things out rigidly across the right space for representation and information, *whatever space that may be*. In particular, surely we can identify an object through some property it alone has, and then go on to make claims about that very object in situations where it may lack the property we used to identify it. Take the example of the previous lecture. I do not (we supposed) have any idea who invented the zip other than that it was a man, but I know enough about the zip to be very confident that whoever invented it is one smart guy. This is how I am sure "The inventor of the zip is one smart guy" is true. And my confidence corresponds to my confidence that the world I am in contains one man who (alone) invented the zip, and he, whoever he is, is smart. I am sure that our world is in the region of logical space where that sentence is true, and nearly all my credence is spread among this set of worlds.

However, I may also want to make claims about how things are with the inventor of the zip in possible situations where he may not be the inventor of the zip. To do this is still to be in the business of providing information, and moreover information about that very person, the inventor of the zip, but it is to do it in a way that allows me to pick the person out in possible situations without presuming he is the inventor of the zip in those situations. To do this, I need a term that picks out the inventor of the zip in possible situations where he may not be, or where he certainly is not, the inventor of the zip. It is plausible that there are a number of ways of doing this, including suitable use of "in fact" or "actually," where these are understood as rigidification devices. Thus, surely I know that the following sentence is true: "Had the man who in fact invented the zip been in the habit of drinking a bottle of scotch before breakfast from the age of 15, he would not have been the inventor of the zip." The obvious explanation of how it is that I know this sentence is true is that I grasp the way that "the man who in fact invented the zip" picks out in all possible worlds the man who invented the zip in our world. The reason I am sure the sentence is true is that I know enough about any at all plausible candidate to be the inventor of the zip in the actual world, that he would be so impaired by that much scotch drinking that he would be unable to invent anything, let alone the zip.

The message is a familiar one. It would be good to have a device for making claims about things one picks out via their being so and so, which allows one to make claims about how they would be if they were not, or possibly were not, so and so. And not only would it be good, we have such devices. I have illustrated one – insert "in fact," understood as a rigidification device – but there are others of course. This tells us that

The man who in fact invented the zip is one smart guy

and

The man who invented the zip is one smart guy

have importantly different meanings. The first but not the second contains a subject term that is good for a certain informational job: ascribing properties to the inventor of the zip in counterfactual cases where he does not, or may not, invent the zip. However, this difference does not affect the role of the two sentences, as they stand, in making claims about how our world is. They represent alike; the situation is like that discussed in the previous lecture. It is obvious that both the inference

> Premise. The man who in fact invented the zip is one smart guy
> Conclusion. The man who invented the zip is one smart guy

and the inference

> Premise. The man who invented the zip is one smart guy
> Conclusion. The man who in fact invented the zip is one smart guy

are trivial; they risk nothing.

However, the two sentences raise exactly the problem that concerned us in the previous lecture. The worlds at which they are true differ markedly. It follows that, for at least one of them, its ir-content is not the set of worlds at which it is true. The culprit is obviously "The man who in fact invented the zip is one smart guy." For, as we noted above, it is plausible that the "The man who invented the zip is one smart guy" represents or gives the information that there is one person, who is a man, who invented the zip, and he's smart, and the worlds at which the sentence is true are the worlds where there is one person, who is a man, who invented the zip, and he is smart. By contrast, the worlds at which "The man who in fact invented the zip is one smart guy" is true are the worlds where the actual inventor of the zip is one smart guy, be he the inventor of the zip at those worlds or not.

The problem going two space was supposed to solve has resurfaced, and it is obvious why. The problem comes from the way language operates across the right space for information and representation, *independently of which space that is*. If the space of the conceptually possible is right for representation and information, we will have sentences whose ir-content differs from the worlds at which they are true, and this will be true regardless of whether or not it is correct to think of the space of the metaphysically possible as a proper subset of the space of the conceptually possible.

We can make essentially the same point by making a simple modification of the stipulated readings of "actual" and "actually" from the previous lecture. There we stipulated that

> "Actually *P*" is true at *w* if and only if "*P*" is true at the actual world.
> "The actual *F* is *G*" is true at *w* if and only if the *F* in the actual world is *G* in *w*.

and noted that, given the above stipulations, "Actually some things are round," for example, has the same ir-content as "Some things are round," despite the set of worlds where the two sentences are true being different. This time around we add to the earlier stipulation that "*w*" ranges over all *conceptually* possible worlds. Then, arguing as in the previous lecture, we get the result that the two sentences have the same ir-content despite not being true at the same conceptually possible worlds. The message is as before. Two spaceism seeks to rescue the idea that ir-content is the set of worlds (or centered worlds) where a sentence is true by going for truth at an especially inclusive set of worlds, the set of conceptually possible worlds conceived of as having the set of metaphysically possible worlds as a proper subset. But if the space of the conceptually possible is the right space for information and representation, there will be sentences with the same ir-content that are not true at the same conceptually possible worlds.

6. Why two spaceism is not a happy home for anti-reductionists

Why is two spaceism popular? My impression is that Lycan is right; in many circles it is pretty much standard doctrine. I hazard that part of the reason is that many see it as promising a way of avoiding reductionist positions in ethics and materialist theories of mind. I will close this lecture by explaining why I think this is a false hope. Although there is a way of using two spaceism to articulate a non-reductionist position in ethics, and on materialism as a theory of mind, in both cases it comes at too high a price.

Let's look at the ethics case first. I will set my remarks against a background that takes the distinction between the non-moral and the moral for granted at the level of language: "right" and "good" are moral terms, "square" and "heavy" are non-moral terms, for instance. The reason I am going to be casual about the distinction is that nothing in what follows hangs on the many good questions that can be asked about the moral–non-moral distinction, and about exactly which terms belong where. What matters for what is to come is that there is a way of making the distinction that ensures that the supervenience of the moral on the non-moral is an important truth. This is widely, though not of course universally, accepted. Also I will be working with the supervenience of the moral on the non-moral in its inter-world or global form, not its intra-world form. So read, it is a thesis about non-morally alike *worlds* being morally alike, not a thesis about non-morally alike items *in* a world being morally alike in that world. Both kinds of supervenience thesis are plausible and widely supported, but it is the first kind that matters for us.

The final preliminary concerns the status of moral terms. I am going to assume that they are descriptive in the sense that their role is to represent how things are, to provide putative information: to say that some action is morally right is to make a claim about how it is. The claim may or may not be, in part or entirely, a claim about how the action is in relation to the speaker, or an idealized version of the speaker, or ... . That issue will not concern us here. The assumption is simply that we should be cognitivists and not expressivists about moral language, and that assumption is perfectly consistent with holding that moral terms serve to report, in part or in whole, our attitudes or our idealized attitudes. In fact we already made the cognitivist assumption in the way we stated the supervenience of the moral on the non-moral. How could it make sense to talk of worlds being morally *alike* unless moral terms were representational?[8]

It follows from the supervenience of the moral on the non-moral that the non-moral necessitates the moral. Any two worlds exactly alike non-morally are exactly alike morally. Once you have fixed the non-moral you have fixed the moral; there is no wriggle room left.

---

[8] For expressivists, supervenience is some kind of consistency constraint on attitudes or acts of valuing or ... required for them to count as ethical ones.

Many find this conclusion strongly counterintuitive: they insist that no matter how much information couched in non-moral terms one may have, it is *always* open to one to jump one way or the other way in coming to a moral verdict. This, they say, is the message of the open question argument and its partner, the argument from the persistence of moral disagreement.

How might they hold onto this intuition, given that global supervenience tells us that that the non-moral necessitates the moral without remainder. Here two spaceism would appear to be an offer too good to refuse. The idea is that we can put matters as follows, drawing on the two-space way of thinking. Any two metaphysically possible worlds that are non-morally exactly alike are morally exactly alike. The non-moral necessitates the moral. But the necessitation is not *a priori* or conceptual. It is conceptually possible to have non-morally alike worlds that differ morally. There are conceptually possible worlds that are alike non-morally but unlike morally. By setting matters in the two-space framework, we can, runs the thought, do justice to global supervenience by granting the necessitation of the moral by the non-moral, at the same time as satisfying the non-reductionist thought behind the open question argument. The moral cannot be reduced to the non-moral but is necessitated by it, as in the view know as Cornell Realism[9] but this kind of view is not restricted to those who self-identify as Cornell realists.[10]

In a way I would like to believe this story. Like many, I feel the force of the open question argument, and we seem to have a neat way to reconcile it with supervenience. But there is, it seems to me, a serious problem. The story is committed to an implausible metaphysics of moral properties reminiscent of Moore (1929).

Let w_a be our world. According to the story, every world w in metaphysically possible space that duplicates our world in non-moral respects – non-morally there is no difference between w_a and w – duplicates our world in moral respects. This follows from the global supervenience of the moral on the non-moral. However, runs the suggestion, there is a world w^* in *conceptually* possible space that duplicates our world in non-moral respects that differs morally from

---

[9]   See, e.g., Brink (1989) and the references therein.

[10] It was the response of many when Simon Blackburn first highlighted the implications of the supervenience of the ethical on the non-ethical, in Blackburn (1971).

our world: w_a and w^* differ in the distribution of moral properties. This is how we respect the non-reductionist idea that the non-moral does not *a priori* entail the moral. But – and here is where the trouble lies – this implies that moral properties are extra properties, additions to the non-moral properties. The moral properties have a property the non-moral properties lack, that of varying as we go from one conceptually possible world to the other.[11] This is a result that would not, I take it, have worried Moore, but it worries me, and I am sure I am not alone in being worried.[12] I, and they, see no reason whatever to believe in such extra properties.

Similar issues arise for two-spaceist attempts to formulate a non-reductive version of materialism.

Materialists about the mind sometimes call themselves physicalists to mark the fact that they are against dual attribute theories of mind as well as substance dualist theories of mind. Their claim is that we are very complex aggregations of items with only physical properties, standing in purely physical relations. How should we delineate the physical properties and relations? This is a good question but not one that I'm going to pursue in any detail. Roughly, the physical properties and relations are of a kind with those that are center stage in current physical science, or are natural descendants of same. Everyone agrees that this rough characterization leaves serious questions open but they are not ones that are germane here. I know that some think that the questions left open cut so deep that there is no interesting doctrine about the mind captured by the label "physicalism." I am going to assume that things aren't that bad. We have a rough and ready grasp of what philosophers mean when they declare themselves to be physicalists about the mind, or so it seems to me and to the many who declare themselves to be physicalists about the mind, and the world more generally.

Physicalists are committed to a supervenience doctrine. If I am nothing more than a complex aggregation of the physical, any

[11] Some object in discussion that independent variation among conceptually possible worlds can only teach us about differences in concepts, not differences in properties. But, in that case, conceptually possible worlds are wrong for information and representation, because information and representation, in the sense engaging us in these lectures, pertain to things and properties, not concepts.

[12] Cornell realists, e.g., typically emphasize that their view is a kind of naturalism that eschews extra properties.

duplicate of me in the sense of being a physical item for item, physical property and relation for physical property and relation duplicate of me, is a psychological duplicate of me. For if I and my duplicate differed psychologically, our psychology would be something over and above our physical natures.[13] It would be that which differed despite all the physical duplication. And this contradicts physicalism about the mind.

None of this is news to most physicalists. Whatever may have been true in the early days of physicalist theories of mind, there is now general agreement among physicalists that the physical way we are necessitates the psychological way we are. Thus the general agreement among physicalists that they have to deny the possibility of zombies: physical duplicates of us that differ from us in lacking consciousness. The disagreement begins when we ask whether we should think of this necessitation as metaphysical (but not conceptual) or as conceptual. Is it like the way, according to the majority, that the distribution of H_2O necessitates the distribution of water, or is it like the way the distribution of objects lighter than I am necessitates the distribution of objects I am heavier than? Is the impossibility of zombies that physicalists are committed to metaphysical but not conceptual, or is it conceptual? Reductionist versions of physicalism, sometimes known as *a priori* physicalism, hold that zombies are conceptually impossible; non-reductionist versions, sometimes known as *a posteriori* physicalism, hold that they are metaphysically impossible but not conceptually impossible.

I have argued elsewhere that physicalists should espouse the reductionist variety of physicalism,[14] but my interest here is more limited. It is to point out that framing matters *in terms of two spaceism* is a bad way to characterize the non-reductionist variety of physicalism.

A non-reductionist who frames matters in the two-space way holds that there is a conceptually possible world, w_z, that is the zombie duplicate of our world, w_a. It is a physical item for item, physical property and relation for physical property and relation, duplicate of

---

[13]   For a comment on how to say this more precisely, see the discussion of (P) in Lecture Five, §4.

[14]   See, e.g., Jackson (1980, 2007a). Here I am at one with Chalmers, see his discussion of *A* type versus *B* type and *C* type versions of materialism in (2002a); see also Lewis (1994).

our world that lacks consciousness. Although throughout metaphysically possible logical space, there are no zombie worlds – you won't find w_z in the space of the metaphysically possible – there are zombie worlds in conceptually possible logical space. But that is inconsistent with physicalism. For w_a is supposed to differ from w_z. But how does it differ from w_z? In having consciousness! But w_a does not differ from w_z in any physical way. Ergo, the point of difference – the consciousness in our world that is absent in w_z – is not a physical way our world is. That contradicts physicalism.

In the ethics case, the two-spaceist way of expressing a non-reductionist position leads to a metaphysical implausibility, at least as we ethical naturalists see things, but one some theorists in ethics are prepared to embrace. In the physicalism case, the two-spaceist way of expressing a non-reductionist position leads to a position that contradicts physicalism.

7. Where to from here?

I have argued that two spaceism is the wrong way to go. But, as we saw in previous lectures, there is a compelling case for holding that some sentences have two contents. It follows that we have no choice but to look for the two contents *within a single logical space*. How might we do this, and what is the right region of that single space to give the ir-content of sentences containing kind names and proper names? That is the business of the next and final lecture. This will allow us to complete the account of the informational value of proper names that we made a start on in the first lecture.

Lecture Five

The Informational Value of Names

1. Where we are

A sentence is a source of information by virtue of making a known partition among possibilities. That has been a recurrent theme of these lectures. It is what lies behind the compelling picture of information as pertaining to the kind of world we occupy. As we have noted a number of times, in some cases it is easy to say what the partition is in terms of truth. "Some things are square" (when asserted) gives us the information that we are in a world where some things are square, and the set of worlds where some things are square is the set of worlds where the sentence is true. But things are not always that simple. The worlds where a sentence is true are not always its ir-content, how it represents things to be.

We saw that in Lecture Two when we noted that some sentences have centered content. They say how a part of a world is in a way that cannot be reduced to saying how a world is. Their content is a set of centered worlds, and thus cannot be a set of worlds, be that set the set where the sentence is true or not. We also saw there that their ir-content is only part of the story about their informational value. A crucial additional part of the story concerns how a linguistic token gives information about the centers of the centered worlds. More on this anon.

In Lecture Three we saw that, even setting aside the issue of centered worlds and centered content, the set of worlds where a sentence is true gets the ir-content of sentences containing "actual" and the like working as rigidification devices, and also sentences containing proper names, demonstrative adjectives, and kind terms, wrong. Indeed, we noted that for some sentences containing, e.g., a mix of names and personal pronouns, sentences for which it makes good intuitive sense that we need centered worlds to capture their ir-content, the set of *centered* worlds where they are true gets their ir-content wrong. Finally, in Lecture Four we saw that an initially attractive attempt to rescue the simple identification of ir-content with the set of worlds, or set of centered worlds, where a sentence is true, by going two space fails. What we need to do in this final lecture is clear. We need to find a set of worlds or centered worlds to be the ir-content of those sentences whose ir-contents are not given by the worlds, or the centered worlds, at which they are true.

But first we need to get clear on how it can be the case that, for some sentences, their ir-content differs from the set of worlds, or centered worlds, where they are true. As we put the puzzle before (Lecture Three, §1), isn't the ir-content nothing other than how a sentence represents things to be, and aren't things being as they are represented to be what it takes to be true? Given that, how can ir-content come apart from the worlds, or centered worlds, where a sentence is true?

What I will do first is describe in the abstract how this can happen. If we have sentences that work a certain way, the separation of ir-content from the worlds or centered worlds where a sentence is true is exactly what we would expect. We will then go on to argue that in English we have sentences that work that way, including those we discussed in Lecture Three. I will mostly talk about sentences containing kind terms and proper names, as they have been the focus of so much attention recently.

2. When truth at a world depends on more than how that world is

A feature of a simple sentence like "Some things are square" is that its truth at a world depends solely on how that world is. Give me a world that contains at least one square thing and you give me a world at which the sentence is true. I do not need to know anything else to know that the sentence is true at that world.

Now suppose we have sentences whose meaning is such that their truth at a world depends on more than how that world is. Their truth also depends in part on how the actual world is. Even if you tell me all there is to know about a world, I cannot in general tell you, in the case of these sentences, whether or not they are true at that world. I need in addition to know how the actual world is. For such sentences, their truth at w depends in a nontrivial way on how w relates to the actual world. Full information about w does not, in itself, allow me to say if they are true at w, because w's relation to w_a also enters the picture, and that is not something full information about w delivers.

If S is such a sentence, then the following is true: the set of worlds, w, at which S is true in general differs from the set of worlds, w, at which S is true *if w is the actual world*. Now the set of worlds, w, at which S is true if w is the actual world is the ir-content of S. We touched on the reason why in Lecture Three, §5. To represent how things are using a sentence is to represent where we might be located in logical space consistent with the truth of the sentence, and those locations are precisely the worlds, w, with the following property: if w is the actual world, the sentence is true. This is because where we might be located is none other than which worlds might be the actual world; the actual world is *our* world. But we have just seen that when S is a sentence whose truth at a world is a nontrivial function of how that world relates to the actual world, the set of worlds, w, at which S is true differs from the set of worlds, w, at which S is true *if w is the actual world*. It follows that, for such sentences, their ir-content is not the set of worlds where they are true.[1]

In short, the ir-content of a sentence is the set of worlds whose actuality is consistent with the truth of the sentence (we will talk shortly about what to say for sentences whose ir-content is a set of centered worlds). This is true for any sentence. What is special about sentences whose truth at a world is a (nontrivial) function of how things actually are is that the set of worlds whose actuality is consistent with the truth of the sentence differs from the set of worlds where the sentence is true.

We can put all this in terms of functions from worlds to truth or falsity. If S is a sentence whose truth at a world is a function both of

---

[1] How come such a sentence is true at these worlds? Isn't a sentence being true at a world a matter of things being the right way at the world? But the right way, for these sentences, is having the way things are standing in the right relation to how they actually are, and that isn't the same as their being how things might actually be, consistent with the truth of the sentence – that's the point. Thanks here to Dan Marshall, but don't hold him responsible.

the world in question and of which world is the actual world, there is a function from $<w', w>$ to T just when S is true at w if w' is the actual world. For any given value of w' – that is, any given designation of some world as the actual world – the function returns a set of worlds such that S is true at those worlds for that value of w'.[2] However, this set will not in general be the set of worlds whose actuality is consistent with the truth of S. That set is instead the set of worlds where the function goes to truth when $w' = w$; the set of worlds at which the sentence is true when that world is the actual world.

Two comments. First, what happens when we need centered worlds to capture ir-content? Much as before but with truth at a world replaced when needed by truth at a centered world. Suppose, that is, that we have sentences whose truth at a centered world $<c, w>$ depends on which centered world is actual. This would mean that I might know all there is to know about that centered world without knowing if the sentence is true at it, because I need to know, in addition, how $<c, w>$ relates to the actual center and world. Suppose, for example, that the sentence is "I have a beard." I cannot say if it is true at $<c, w>$ unless I know whether the actual producer of the sentence has a beard. If c produced the sentence at the actual world, then it is true at $<c, w>$ just if c has a beard in w, and is false otherwise. Or suppose that the sentence is "I actually have a beard." In this case I cannot say if it is true at $<c, w>$ unless I know whether the actual producer of the sentence has a beard at the actual world. But what I do know, for both sentences, is the set of centered worlds whose actuality is consistent with the truth of the sentence. That set is the set of centered worlds $<c, w>$ where c has a beard in w.

The second comment is directed to a question that sometimes comes up in discussion concerning how to connect what I am saying with the literature, with its focus on functions from sentences, worlds, and centered worlds, into truth values. The literature typically talks of there being two functions. One determines the primary intension, the other the secondary intension. The first goes from a sentence and a world or, more often, a centered world, to a truth value – it

---

[2] These are the rows, one of which is the horizontal proposition, in Stalnaker's (1999a) terms. The horizontal proposition is the row you get when w' = the actual world.

determines the primary intension of the sentence; the second goes from a sentence and a world (never, to my knowledge, a centered world) to a truth value – it determines the secondary intension of the sentence.[3] In our terms, the ir-content of a sentence is the primary intension of the sentence *provided and only provided* that the function from worlds or centered worlds is understood as described above. Only on that understanding – the understanding that makes the primary intension the set of worlds or centered worlds whose actuality is consistent with the sentence's truth – is the primary intension the same as ir-content. Without that understanding, the primary intension is just another set of worlds or centered worlds with no special claim to be how a sentence represents things to be.[4] But let me labor the point with a simple example that does not involve centering. Take the sentence "The actual tallest person is the heaviest person," where "actual" is stipulated to operate as explained in Lecture Three (and see §4, below). That is to say, its truth at w is a function of how w is and which world is the actual world, according to the rule: it is true at w if and only if the tallest person at the actual world is the heaviest at w. We can now ask, of each world w, what truth value the sentence takes if that world is the actual world. The answer will be that the sentence is true just if the tallest person at w is the heaviest person at w. If the primary intension is understood as the set of worlds w where the sentence is true at w if w is the actual world, then it (the primary intension) is the ir-content of the sentence. (And notice that the set in question will be the set of worlds where the tallest person is the heaviest person, which is the intuitively right answer.)

3. A diagram to give the key idea

The talk in the preceding section of functions from worlds to truth values, and from centered worlds to truth values, and of how the value of the functions may vary depending on which world, or which

---

[3]   Chalmers (2002b) talks of epistemic and subjunctive rather than primary and secondary intensions.

[4]   This is why, in the past, I have preferred to talk of A-intensions rather than primary intensions.

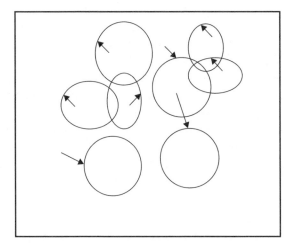

Figure 5.1

centered world, is actual can have a 'glazing' effect. Functions are not very 'folk friendly'. The same material can be seen in figure 5.1.

Here is how to read the diagram for some given sentence *S*, starting with the case where *S*'s ir-content is a set of centered worlds. The rectangle in that case is the logical space of centered worlds. (We can still talk of a set of worlds in this space, meaning a set of centered worlds, alike in world but taking every possible value as center.) For each *S* there is a set of arrows. The circle at the tip of each arrow gives the set of worlds where *S* is true if the centered world at the origin of the arrow is the actual centered world. Thus, if the origin of some given arrow is <*c*, *w*> and *S* is "I have a beard," the tip of the arrow is the set of worlds where *c* has a beard. If *S* is "I actually have a beard," then the tip of the arrow is the set of worlds where *c* has a beard in *w*. The ir-content of *S* is the set of origins of arrows whose tips go to circles that enclose their origins. Those origins are the set of centered worlds whose actuality is consistent with the truth of *S*. The secondary intension (horizontal proposition) of *S* is the set of worlds at the tip of the arrow whose origin is the actual centered world. Thus, if *S* is "I have a beard," said by me, the secondary intension is the set of worlds where *FJ* has a beard, and if *S* is "I actually have a beard," said by me, the secondary intension is the set of worlds containing *FJ* (as I do in fact have a beard).

The story is much the same but a bit simpler if S's ir-content is a set of worlds. The rectangle is then the logical space of worlds. The circle at the tip of each arrow gives the set of worlds where S is true if the world at the origin is the actual world. If S is, say, "Something is round," the circle at the tip of each arrow will be the same set of worlds – those where something is round – no matter what the origin is. If S is, say, "The actual F is G," the circle at the tip of each arrow will vary depending on its origin; for each origin, it will be the set of worlds, w, where the F in the origin world is G in w. In either case, S's ir-content is the set of origins of arrows for S, whose tips go to circles that enclose their origins.

4. A language where truth at a world is, by stipulation, a function of which world is actual

We have seen how and why the ir-content for a sentence can diverge from the worlds or centered worlds at which it is true. But what I offered was essentially a possibility proof. *If* there are sentences whose truth at w is a function of which world or centered world is actual, we will have the noted divergence and be able to explain it. But are there any such sentences in English? Yes. In fact, in the discussion of "I have a beard" and "I actually have a beard," I presumed in both cases that, and how, their truth at a centered world is a function of how things actually are. But let's start by looking at how things shape up for a simple fragment of 'stipulated English'; English embellished with the terms "actual," "actually," and the like, operating in the way we illustrated in Lecture Three. There we stipulated as follows:

> "Actually P" is true at w if and only if "P" is true at the actual world.
> "The actual F is G" is true at w if and only if the F in the actual world is G in w.

Given these stipulations, it is obvious that, for example, "Actually some things are round" and "The actual President of the United States is left-handed" are sentences whose truth at a world is a function both of how the world is and of which world is the actual world.

Perhaps I should emphasize that this is a property of the stipulated *meanings*. Sometimes it is suggested that what is meant – indeed, all that can be meant – by talk of the way the truth value of a sentence at a world can vary as we vary which world is the actual world, is the way the truth value of a sentence depends in part on what it means. The contention is that variation in truth value of a sentence at some given world as we vary which world is actual, is nothing more than variation induced by the fact that what the sentence means is a function of how things actually are. In varying the world taken to be the actual world, we vary what the sentence means, and that is where the second dimension of truth dependence comes from.[5] However, the variation we are talking about is a product of the meanings the example sentences *in fact have*. Given what they in fact mean, their truth at a given world varies as we vary which world is actual. For example, anyone who understands the clauses for "actually" and "actual" given in the preceding paragraph is able to chart the way the truth values of the sentences in the clauses are a function of two variables. In doing this, they work with the given understanding of the sentences; they don't change the way they understand them as we go through the various cases.

Moreover, the practice of philosophers themselves in other contexts tells us we have no trouble understanding variation in truth value for a sentence under variation in which world is the actual world, while keeping the meanings of the words constant – that is, as they actually are. Take a claim of a kind often discussed in the philosophy of mind

(P) Any world exactly like the *actual* world in all physical respects (and with no gratuitous additions) is exactly like the actual world in all psychological respects.[6]

Those who affirm (P) do so because they have a certain view about the nature of our world; those who deny it have a different view. The

---

[5] See, e.g., Lycan (2009, p. 71). He describes this as his "guess" at what might be meant by something "obscure and vexed."

[6] The reason for the proviso in parenthesis is that physicalists typically, and rightly in my view, allow that we might duplicate our (purely physical, in their view) world physically and yet change psychology, by *adding* 'angels' with rich psychological lives realized in non-physical stuff.

parties to the dispute agree about the right truth value to give the sentence under various hypotheses about which world is the actual world. They agree that if the actual world is one of the worlds where physicalism is true, (P) is true; and that if the actual world is one of the worlds where dualism is true, (P) is false. Their disagreement is over the nature of the actual world. And as they consider the different hypotheses about the nature of the actual world, they are not changing the meanings of the words. When they discuss the way (P)'s truth value is a function of which world is actual, they take it for granted that the words "physical," "alike," "psychological," etc. are given their actual meanings, and draw on their grasp of those meanings in deciding, for each hypothesis about the nature of the actual world, whether (P) is true or false under that hypothesis.

5. On looking for examples of two-dimensional sentences in the English of the folk

The sentences we have just been discussing are two-dimensional in the sense that their truth at a world is in part also a function of which world is actual. We stipulated meanings for "actual" and "actually" that ensured this. We noted in passing that "I have a beard," with the meaning it in fact has in English, is pretty obviously two-dimensional in the sense that the worlds at which it is true are a function of how things actually are, in particular of who in fact produces it, and we said the same for "I actually have a beard" (in this second case, truth at a world depends both on who in fact produces it and whether they in fact have a beard). How widespread in English, our English, are sentences that are two-dimensional? This is the same question as, How widespread are sentences whose ir-content is not the set of worlds or centered worlds where they are true but is instead the set of worlds or centered worlds whose actuality is consistent with their truth?

The first thing to say is that it makes perfect sense that there should be a good number of such sentences. They expand our representational powers. We saw an example in the previous lecture, but it bears repeating. Suppose I know that one man invented the zip but have no idea who he is. If I want to make some categorical claim about him, it does not matter whether I use, say, "The man who invented the zip is one smart guy" or "The man who in fact invented the zip is one smart guy." We labored that point. But suppose I want to make claims about him in counterfactual situations where he may not be the inventor of the zip. How do I solve the problem of picking him out to be a subject of predication in situations where he may lack the only identifying property available to me? As we said in the previous lecture, the obvious solution is to exploit the fact that there *is* an identifying property available to me. In every world w, I can identify him as the person who invented the zip in the actual world. It makes sense that we should have an easy way of exploiting this fact and, plausibly, using "The man who in fact invented the zip" is that way. Thus we understand "Had the man who in fact invented the zip been in the habit of drinking a bottle of scotch before breakfast from the age of 15, he would not have been the inventor of the zip" in a way that makes it true, by asking, of the man in the actual world, how he would be in worlds where he drank a bottle of scotch before breakfast from the age of 15, and judging that, in the closest such world, he would not have invented the zip.[7] And when we debate the truth or falsity of this sentence, its two-dimensional nature is very much in play. We use what we know about the actual world and especially the likely alcoholic capacity of whoever invented the zip in the actual world, to assess the likelihood of his inventing the zip in the closest worlds where he drinks all that scotch from the age of 15.

The upshot is that the way "The man who in fact invented the zip" works in the discussion above is exactly the way "The man who actually invented the zip" works, on the stipulation about how "actually" works. We introduced "actual" and "actually" as stipulations to make the point in the abstract that there might be sentences whose truth at a world is a function both of how that world is and of how the actual world is, and to avoid distractions arising from the sometime use in English of such terms as emphasis markers, but it is clear that there are, as a matter of fact, uses in English of terms like "actual," "actually," "in fact," etc. which work, or work on occasion, in the way we stipulated "actual" and "actually" to work. What is more, we have seen that there is a clear rationale for why our language should have terms that work this way.

---

[7] I express the point in terms of a simple version of the possible worlds analysis of counterfactuals. Nothing hangs on the simplification.

But what about proper names and names of kinds? "Plato" and "water" do not contain occurrences of "in fact," "actual," etc. We will discuss them separately. What we will see is that, although they do not contain explicit rigidification devices, the way they work is to pick out items in other possible worlds via their relation to how things are in the actual world in a way that makes them rigid desig-nators – or, rather, that is how proper names work and how names of kinds often work. This is why the worlds at which sentences con-taining them are true differ from the worlds, or centered worlds, whose actuality is consistent with their truth – the second of course being their ir-content. The phenomenon of centering will make the discussion slightly (*slightly*) more complex. I will discuss names of kinds first, sticking with the old warhorse "water," and later proper names. As I have already hinted, there is a major difference between them. First, however, we need to note some points about methodology.

6. How should we approach questions like, How do we use the word "water"? and, How do we use the word "Gödel"?

From the informational-representational perspective of these lectures, what is central is what people are saying about how things are when they use "water" and "Gödel" in sentences like "There is water nearby" and "Gödel lived in Princeton." For the question of how someone uses a word in the sense of central interest to us is nothing other than the question of how they represent things to be when using the word assertorically.

This question is in part an empirical one about how people use the words in question and, like most philosophers, I have not carried out carefully designed surveys. This does not mean that I am not entitled to any opinion at all on the subject. The word "water" is in general use and that gives me, and competent English speakers in general, quite a lot of empirical information on how people use the word. Also, I know something about how I use the word, and although we should be cautious about extrapolating too confidently from our own case, to the extent that I am entitled to hold that my usage is typical, it gives me some useful information about how others use the word "water" – defeasible information, as reflection on the need for double blind experiments in drug trials reminds us (but I needed Simon Cullen to remind me).

The empirical side of the story is important in connection with an observation Kripke makes in the course of his attack on the description theory of reference for proper names. He notes that someone might determine the reference of "Gödel" by saying "By 'Gödel' I shall mean the man, whoever he is, who proved the incompleteness of arithmetic," and goes on to say "… you can do this if you want to. There's nothing really preventing it. You can just stick to that determination. If that's what you do, then if Schmidt discovered the incompleteness of arithmetic you *do* refer to him when you say 'Gödel did such and such'" (1980, p. 91). We should agree with Kripke. The only query we might raise is why he includes the word "really." There is nothing at all preventing us using "Gödel" that way. But, as Kripke says immediately after the passage quoted above, "But that's not what most of us do." How was Kripke able to be so confident, for there are no reports of surveys of word usage in *Naming and Necessity*?

There are three reasons Kripke was able to be so confident. First, Kripke carried out a kind of survey. He described a possible case in which someone called "Schmidt" proves the incompleteness of arithmetic and Gödel steals the glory, but in which we have no inclination whatever to say that "Gödel" refers to Schmidt. It is an empirical fact that we, or anyway an awful lot of us, have no inclination to say that, in the described case, "Gödel" refers to Schmidt. Kripke was carrying out a survey in the same way that Gettier was with his counter-examples to knowledge being true justified belief, and Putnam was with the Twin Earth example.[8] In all three cases it is an important empirical fact that tells us something about word usage that there was substantial agreement that Schmidt isn't Gödel, that Smith's belief that the man who will get the job has 10 coins in his pocket isn't knowledge (although it is a case of true justified belief), and that XYZ on Twin Earth isn't water.[9]

---

[8]   Gettier (1963); Putnam (1975)

[9]   Though, as we will note shortly, the agreement in the case of Twin Earth is not as solid as in the other cases.

Secondly, Kripke knew enough about some speakers of English to know that they used "Gödel" to refer to Gödel when they knew nothing whatever about incompleteness, in which case it was very unlikely they were using "Gödel," or indeed any word, for the person who proved the incompleteness of arithmetic. Finally, Kripke knew enough about the way very many people used names to know that there was an alternative account of how we use "Gödel" that has the signal advantage of explaining why proper names are so useful. I mean the account we discussed and supported in the first lecture, the account which views names like "Gödel" as conduits of knowledge and information deriving from a baptism in the past.

These reasons, taken together, make a very strong, empirical case that we don't use "Gödel" for the person who proved the incompleteness of arithmetic. The case is defeasible. If some philosophers sailing under the banner of experimental philosophy carry out well-designed surveys that produce strong evidence that some group or other do use "Gödel" for the person who proved the incompleteness of arithmetic, then we should restrict the "we" of the first sentence of this paragraph. I am sure this group, if it exists, do not use the word the way the vast majority (myself included) use "Gödel," but this does not stop *them* using the word for the person who proved the incompleteness of arithmetic.

There is, however, something that surveys cannot show. They cannot show that, for some group, the description theory of reference for proper names is true whereas, for some other group, the causal theory is true. The surveys we are talking about consist of soliciting responses to vignettes. Subjects are presented with short, or sometimes not so short, descriptions of possible cases and invited to say who if anyone N is, or sometimes who if anyone does "N" refer to. However, because the cases are *described*, there is no question of their delivering ammunition against the description theory of reference for proper names. What they may do, and in my view do do, is provide evidence that for some groups the key descriptions are certain causal descriptions.[10]

---

[10]   Here I am dissenting from Machery et al. (2008). They report experimental results that they describe as suggesting the some groups have a "causal-historical view" of reference whereas other groups have a "descriptivist" view of reference. But the experiments they detail support at most differences over the descriptions that fix reference.

The point here is essentially the one we made in the first lecture. The causal theory of reference for proper names is not the same as causal descriptivism. The second is a version of the description theory, whereas the causal theory of reference is the view, in effect, that the only thing wrong with causal descriptivism is that it holds that the folk know the causal descriptions that determine the reference of a name like "Feynman" or "Mark Twain." The folk don't know them. To which we objected (in the first lecture), in that case, why aren't the folk ringing the philosophy department for advice when they are asked to work on, say, finding the historical Helen of Troy for a television series or a book?

7. More on the evidential role of intuitions about possible cases

The remarks of the previous few paragraphs will rightly be read as friendly toward experimental philosophy. I am seeing the work of experimental philosophers as part of a well-credentialed tradition in philosophy of consulting intuitions about possible cases. Some wonder about the credentials of this tradition. As Devitt says in a recent paper (forthcoming), "We don't do physics, biology, or economics simply by consulting people's intuitions. Why should semantics be different?"

He is not suggesting, I take it, that we do philosophy without appeal to thought experiments and intuitions about them. There are questions that cannot be addressed sensibly in the absence of reflections on, intuitions about, possible cases. Take, for example, the central question in ethics about the contribution equity makes to value. We all agree that typically equitable distributions of goods are better than inequitable ones (while quarreling about what "equitable" means here). The real action starts when we ask if being equitable is a value in itself, or whether the value of equity is founded on the way it typically makes things go better. In order to address that question, we need to ask questions like, Is a world with exactly the same amount of the good as our world but more equitably distributed, better than our world? And you don't – cannot – answer that question by carrying out experiments on that non-actual world. That's an impossibility.

What is more, intuitions about possible cases are ubiquitous outside philosophy. Discussions of voting systems, possible taxation changes, the advisability of invading Iraq or of letting Lehman Brothers go to the wall, are replete with claims about what would or might have happened if so and so, and these are claims about possible cases. The question Devitt is putting on the table is not, Should we do away with thought experiments and intuitions about possible cases? but, How and when is it justified to use them?

The short answer to this question is that it is a case-by-case matter. There is no uniform story to be told about the role of reflection about possible cases in intellectual enquiry.[11] However, our interest here is in one role. Intuitions about possible cases can provide important information about the cases we use a word for – and here we connect with Devitt's focus on semantics. This should be no surprise. The word will be one of our words, and our opinion about the cases we use the word for should be respected by all except skeptics about speakers' knowledge of what their words mean. This, then, is why I think we should be tolerant about differences in reactions to the vignettes when (*when*) they are best thought of as providing information on the cases we use one or another word for, provided of course that the vignettes are presented in a way that passes the tests for a good social science survey.[12] The differences need not show that one group must be wrong; they may simply reveal a difference in how certain terms are being used.

When are reactions to vignettes best thought of as providing information on the cases we use a word for? When enough information is provided in the vignette, when the user of the word grants that they have all the information that is relevant. If I tell John Doe a story in which a house sells for $400,000 and ask him for his opinion as to whether the house sold for above or below the median price for some suburb, his answer will be driven by what he thinks my words mean, including the word "median," *and* what he thinks other houses in the suburb sold for. But if I tell him all there is to know about what other houses in the suburb sold for, and he agrees that that gives him all the information he could possibly need, his answer will

---

[11]   For a bit more detail on the lack of uniformity, see Jackson (2009b).
[12]   For discussion of the importance of good methodology in collecting intuitive responses to vignettes, see Cullen (2010).

most likely tell me what he means by "median" – most likely and not certainly, because it is always possible that one of us has made some kind of processing error.

It is now time to look at the case of the word "water," asking if it is two dimensional and what its ir-content might be, or better, what the ir-content of sentences containing it like "There is water nearby," might be.

8. What information do we impart with the word "water" – first pass

I cannot give a definitive answer for all users of the word "water." As I say above, I haven't done the legwork. The same goes for nearly all philosophers writing about the meaning of the word "water" and natural kind terms in general. And it turns out that this matters; indeed, it matters a lot. A number of key claims philosophers make about the word "water" require empirical support. Although they are presented as philosophical theses in the sense of theses that can be defended using materials available in the philosophy seminar room, they in fact need additional empirical research.

The example we will focus on are the various doctrines about the way the reference of the word "water" varies with the speaker's environment. Whether they are true or false depends on facts about word usage that are not common knowledge. In this regard the situation is different from the one that faced Kripke when he insisted that most of us don't use "Gödel" for the person who proved the incompleteness of arithmetic. Although this is an empirical claim about word usage, it is, as we noted, one Kripke had very good evidence for, especially after he garnered responses to the Schmidt case. But, as we will see, the key facts about the usage of "water" are not nearly as accessible.

This does not mean that the word "water" is informationally useless, that how we represent things to be when we say "There is water nearby" is obscure and variable across different speakers of English to an extent that threatens its usefulness. It means that there is variation among speakers in ways that are not common knowledge, but, as we will observe, the variations aren't big enough or important enough to matter much in practice. They matter for various philosophical theses about the reference of the word "water" in possible cases, but not for the survival value of hearing the word in, say, the sentences "There is water one mile due north" and "Be careful, the water is hot." How different speakers represent things to be varies in ways we don't know but not in ways that matter for day-to-day needs.

There is, however, a part of our use of "water" that is pretty much common knowledge. We use it to tell about a kind of stuff we're acquainted with that is typically, though far from always, potable, odorless, and colorless, and which falls from the sky and fills the oceans and rivers – the watery stuff as it is often tagged. This is why the sentence "Water = H_2O" is a good sentence to tell people about an exciting discovery about our world, namely, the discovery that the watery stuff is H_2O. This is why dictionary entries in effect define "water" as the watery stuff. This why hearing "There is water one mile due north" has survival value: most of us know that it tells where some watery stuff is, and that's good news for those lost in a desert.

However, these remarks about how we use the word "water" leave a lot open, and the matters they leave open are precisely the ones that can only be closed by doing the legwork, and maybe doing the legwork will only close some of them in the sense that it will tell us that there is one degree or other of indeterminacy in how we use the word "water." What the remarks leave open does not matter in real life, which is why no harm is done, but they do matter for some widely discussed theses about the referential behavior of the word, theses most often raised via the Twin Earth parable, as I said earlier. Let's now detail some of this.

The remarks leave open, for instance, whether or not "water" is rigid. They leave open, that is, whether or not, in the other possible world version of Twin Earth – the version in which Twin Earth is another possible world that cannot be differentiated by its inhabitants from the actual world but which has XYZ as the watery stuff (imagine that the time is before the key experiments on Earth that revealed that the watery stuff is H_2O, and the key experiments on Twin Earth that revealed that their watery stuff is XYZ) – "water" refers to XYZ. Many current analytical philosophers have the strong intuition that XYZ on Twin Earth, in its other possible worlds version, is not water, and more generally that water is H_2O, the actual watery stuff, at every possible world where it exists, and accordingly that "water" is rigid. I have been going along with this majority view. This is why I took it, in Lecture Three, that "There is water nearby" and "There is H_2O nearby" are true at the very same worlds. This strong intuition tells us something about how these analytical philosophers use the word "water." But this is consistent with others using "water" as short for the non-rigid "the watery stuff"; there's nothing stopping them. I know many insist that the Twin Earth parable tells us something fundamental about the very nature of reference and not something about the way we use words: "water" has to refer to H_2O in the other possible world version of Twin Earth, the very nature of reference requires it. But that cannot be right. It is undeniable that we could use "water" non-rigidly, albeit in a way that meant it co-referred in our world with "water" as used rigidly.

How, as a matter of fact, do others use the word? I use it so that "water" is rigid. I know enough about my word usage to know that. I also know that this is, at least in part, a conscious decision in the interests of bringing my usage into line with most of my colleagues. My experience with students, and others report similar results, is that there is a division of opinion. Some say that of course XYZ isn't water; others say that water is multiply realizable (especially if they are polled after the lecture on functionalism in the philosophy of mind) and that the Twin Earth case makes this vivid. What is more, there is no convergence as the debate proceeds. By way of contrast, when I discuss Gettier cases with students, there is convergence, upon reflection, on the view that they are not cases of knowledge.

What else, apart from rigidity, is left open by what is pretty much common knowledge about how we use the word "water"? Two matters especially. First, do we use "water" for *the* watery stuff, so that if there are two watery kinds in the actual world, "water" doesn't refer? Secondly, what is the ambit of the acquaintance clause? What constraint precisely does it impose? The interplay between possible answers to these two questions drives the way the reference of "water" depends on speakers' environments. The simplest way to see this is with a concrete example.

Suppose that Fred uses "water" at time *t* to refer to *the* kind of stuff *he's been acquainted with for the last 20 minutes* that is typically though far from always potable, odorless, and colorless, and which falls from the sky and fills the oceans and rivers. He makes this clear by an act of stipulation, and we have every reason to believe him. Now consider the following version of the remote part of the actual world version of the Twin Earth parable. Fred is a competent English speaker who has lived for 20 years on Earth. It is before the experiments on Earth that showed that the typically potable, odorless, clear, river-filling stuff, etc. on Earth is H_2O. Twin Earth is a remote planet superficially indistinguishable from Earth, where the typically potable, odorless, clear, river-filling stuff, etc. is XYZ. It is before the experiments on Twin Earth that showed this stuff to be XYZ. Fred is drugged and taken to Twin Earth. When he wakes he has no idea that he has been moved away from Earth. He in consequence uses the word "water" for the potable, odorless, clear, river-filling stuff, etc. he comes across. What do his initial uses of "water" on Twin Earth (not that he knows that he's on Twin Earth) refer to? And does the reference of "water" in his mouth change at some point in his new life on Twin Earth?

Questions like these have been matters of lively debate.[13] But given the stipulation concerning Fred's usage, there is no room for debate in the case of the word as he uses it. The answers follow from the stipulation. For the first 20 minutes (or maybe a bit less to allow for the time he was drugged) on Twin Earth his use of "water" fails to refer. This is because there is no such stuff as *the* kind he's been acquainted with for the last 20 minutes. There have been two kinds. Once the 20 minutes is up, his use of "water" refers unequivocally to XYZ. And of course Fred could change the answer by changing his stipulation. And of course he could make the answers vague to one degree or another by being vague to one degree or another in how he uses the word "water." And of course the same goes for us.

What is the moral? It is that how the reference of "water" changes as speakers move their location between Earth and Twin Earth depends on how speakers use words. This means we cannot answer questions about possible changes in reference without that information. What is more, I think it is clear we do not have the needed information, at least as far as the typical English speaker is concerned. We can always stipulate in our own case of course, and thus make one or another answer correct – for us at the time of the stipulation

---

[13]   Much of it prompted by Burge (1988).

anyway. As I indicate above, I think we probably know enough about how the typical English speaker uses the word "water" to be able to say that acquaintance comes into it, and that being of a kind that is typically potable, river-filling and all the rest come into it, but there is no precision in what we know, and maybe no precision there to be found. For consider the following raft of possible uses:

(i) A typical English speaker uses "water" at time t to refer to *the kind of stuff they've been acquainted with for the last 20 minutes* that is typically though far from always potable, odorless, and colorless, falls from the sky and which fills the oceans and rivers.

(ii) A typical English speaker uses "water" at time t to refer to *any kind of stuff they've been acquainted with for the last year* that is typically though far from always potable, odorless, and colorless, and which falls from the sky and fills the oceans and rivers.

(iii) A typical English speaker uses "water" at time t to refer to *the only kind of stuff they've been acquainted with up to now* that is typically though far from always potable, odorless, and colorless, and which falls from the sky and fills the oceans and rivers.

...

Surely we have no idea which is correct for a given speaker of English, and plausibly there would be little point in carrying out polls. The people being polled would think the matter too unimportant to make, or have made, a decision about. We would plausibly merely get evidence that the matter was, for the folk, indeterminate.[14] Although the differences between the various possibilities listed above can make big differences to what "water" refers to in one or another Twin Earth scenario, they make no difference in real life. Twin Earth doesn't exist and there is only one kind that comes anywhere near being typically potable, river-filling, etc., and it is the kind we are acquainted with throughout our lives.

There are two more variations in possible uses of "water" we should comment on. First, I assumed, in plenty of company, that acquaintance is part of the story about how we, most of us, use

---

[14] As Lewis (1994) says.

"water." I assumed we use the word for the, or a, kind that is typically though far from always potable, odorless, and colorless, falls from the sky and which fills the oceans and rivers, with which we are acquainted. We have been discussing various ways the acquaintance clause might be made precise and *inter alia* the impact of one or another precisification on how the reference of "water" does or doesn't change upon transport between Earth and Twin Earth (thought of here and below as a remote part of our world). That there is an acquaintance clause of some kind or another is crucial to ensuring that "water" in the mouth of a stay at home Fred, one who lives all his life on Earth, refers to H_2O but not to XYZ. It is Fred's being acquainted with H_2O but not XYZ (maybe via his language community's being acquainted with H_2O but not XYZ) that ensures that the reference of "water" in his mouth is to H_2O but not to XYZ. Provided, and only provided, there is an acquaintance clause – that is, provided and only provided Fred uses "water" to say how certain stuff he is acquainted with is – are matters as Putnam (1975) said in the article that introduced the Twin Earth parable to the philosophical community. However, there is nothing stopping Fred from using "water" for the, or a, kind that is typically though far from always potable, odorless, and colorless, falls from the sky and fills the oceans and rivers, without any requirement that he be acquainted with it. In that case, in Fred's mouth the reference of "water" in the Twin Earth parable will depend on whether Fred uses the word for *the* or *a* kind that is typically but far from always potable, odorless, and colorless, and which falls from the sky and fills the oceans and rivers, and in neither case will it be true that "water" refers to H_2O and fails to refer to XYZ. If he uses it for *the* kind, then in the Twin Earth case "water" refers neither to H_2O nor to XYZ. There is no unique kind. If he uses it for *a* kind, then in the Twin Earth case "water" refers to *both* H_2O and to XYZ.

Secondly, I assumed, perhaps in less company, that it is common knowledge that we use the word "water" for a (normally liquid) kind that is typically though far from always potable, odorless, and colorless, and which falls from the sky and fills the oceans and rivers, or typically has a good number of these properties. I took it, for instance, that stuff of a kind that never had any of these properties did not count as water, as the folk use the word "water." I am sure this is true for how I use the word "water." However, others deny this and invite us to contemplate the following kind of story.[15] We discover that the stuff we take to be a kind that is typically potable, etc., is, as it might be, made of tiny pink granules. Although the granules are pink, when assembled their pinkness is masked and they appear to make up a single colorless liquid. But it isn't really a liquid. The granules "flow" at room temperature in the way fine sand does and so trick us into thinking that an assembly of them at room temperature is a liquid, properly speaking. These granules play no role in sustaining life. What sustains life is an invisible vapor that surrounds them. And so it goes.

We could discover this. Very, very unlikely but possible. *I* would announce this discovery using the word "water," in, as it might be, "Incredibly, it turns out there is no water." I think that this is how the folk would announce it and that we would introduce a word, as it might be, "granulum," for the stuff we had taken to be water, but I cannot be sure of course. I haven't done the legwork. Some philosophers insist that they would describe the discovery using the word "water" in, as it might be, "We have discovered that water isn't any of things we thought it was; it is an assembly of tiny pink granules, etc." I see no reason not to believe them. But I don't believe them if they go on to suggest that it is what we would *all* do, or that it is the *only right* thing to do, or what we *must* do. I know that they, like me, have not done the legwork. Their confidence tells me that *they* use the word "water" for, as it might be, the, or a, kind that is *taken* to be typically though far from always potable, odorless, and colorless, etc. It tells us nothing though about how others use the word.

In one sense we would have here a very big difference in how things are being represented to be by this just discussed use of the word "water." In another sense the difference is trivial. How likely is it that the kind we *take* to be typically though far from always potable, odorless, and colorless, etc. is not in fact the kind that *is* typically though far from always potable, odorless, and colorless, etc? Miniscule.

The upshot of our review of how various people do or might use the word "water" in ways that would not be obviously deviant (the

---

[15] For a recent example, see Tye (2009, p. 58). (Of course, a user of the word "water" had better not say that *any* discovery about *x* is consistent with *x*'s being water, as they use the word. They need to allow for the possibility of discovering that *x* is *not* water.)

differences would not show up in practice unless they did philosophy of language) is that the information delivered by the use of "water" is unclear (it varies from person to person but in ways we don't know) or vague. But this does not matter. There will be some unclarity or vagueness about exactly which possibilities are as some use of "There is water nearby" represents things to be, but the regions of unclarity or vagueness will concern worlds that have almost no chance of being the actual world. They will be in the 'don't care' category.

9. With enemies like these, who needs friends?[16]

I know some will want to insist about now, or maybe they have been wanting to insist for some pages, that although the remarks about possible diversity in the way we use "water" are all well and good, I have consistently failed to do justice to the fundamental insight lying behind Putnam's work, especially. It is the scientifically significant *kind* that matters. All the to-ing and fro-ing about being watery, however one spells out the details, misses the key point that being watery and all that, the superficial properties, the properties the folk have known about for centuries, are mere folk markers or identification intuitions, which serve to identify stuff that might possibly be water.[17] They deliver an initial division into water and non-water. We then investigate how well this typing corresponds to that made in terms of the categories of our best science, and it is *these categories* that settle whether or not some stuff is water. If best science and its categories vindicate the 'folk' typing in sufficiently many cases and nearly enough (whatever precisely that comes to), *x* is water if and only if *x* belongs to the right category, or one of the right categories, as discerned by best science; if it does not, there is no such stuff as water. Either way, it is our best science, not the folk markers or identification intuitions, that settles the issue.

This is exactly the style of view I have been outlining. The rhetorical presentation makes it sound different but it isn't in reality. The

---

[16]   This is the title of an album by Fred Frith and Henry Kaiser.

[17]   My discussion here (and elsewhere) is indebted to discussions with David Braddon-Mitchell. I take the term "identification intuition" from Devitt (1996, p. 73). In his view, the relevant intuitions sometimes are those of the folk but sometimes are those of one or another body of experts.

view just outlined can be summarized as follows: (a) water exists if and only if there is a scientific kind, K, that matches, near enough, to the folk typing, and (b) x is water if and only if x belongs to that kind. This means that x is water if and only if x belongs to the or a kind that has what it takes to match, near enough, to the folk typing. Just the kind of position I have been saying is the common core to our use of "water."

What deceives is the rhetoric about the kind discerned by science settling whether or not some stuff is water. The kind only does this *if* water exists, and water exists just if there is a kind discerned by science matching, near enough, to the folk typing, a kind to which x must belong to be water.

10. What information do we impart with the word "water" – second pass

We used sentences containing "water" in Lecture Three to illustrate the fact that for some sentences, their ir-content differs from the worlds at which they are true. This required us to make the usual assumption that "water" is a rigid designator. But, as we note in the preceding section but one, rigidity, while no doubt a feature of many uses of the word, mine included, does not have to be true of all uses. I know this relaxed attitude is anathema to many. They insist that rigidity isn't an option to be taken up or declined. It is a deep fact about the way reference to kinds works, and maybe reference in general, and is something we learn from reflections inspired by Kripke and Putnam on the connection between causation and reference. To which I reply, (i) Where is the *bar* on using "water" as a shorthand for the watery kind? And (ii) causation is neutral as between H_2O and the, or a, watery stuff as the reference of "water." How could that fail to be the case given Leibniz's law? H_2O *is* the watery stuff. If the claim is, rather, that the feature that gets tracked is its being H_2O and not its being the watery stuff, that seems as a matter of fact false. What guides us in our use of "water" is our belief that some stuff is the watery kind; it is certainly what guided people in times when no one knew that water was H_2O.

But we can set this disagreement aside when we ask, How do we get the ir-content of "water" sentences right in terms of truth at worlds on the presumption that "water" is rigid? We can ask that question without taking a stand on the source of the presumption, which is essentially where the disagreement lies. And we answer the question following the schema laid out early in this lecture (in §2): replace the question, At which worlds is, say, "There is water somewhere" true? by the question, Which worlds or centered worlds are such that their being the actual world or centered world is consistent with the truth of "There is water somewhere"? It is the answer to the second that gives ir-content. For as we said in §2, to represent that things are thus and so is to mark out the worlds or centered worlds that might be actual consistent with the truth of what is said. Which worlds or centered worlds are these? The answer will vary from rigid use to rigid use, depending on the details. But here is how it looks on one spelling out of the details, a spelling out that seems to me to be close to how many use the word and is of a kind with one of the usages mentioned above. (It is how I use the word, for what that is worth.)

On this use, "water" in X's mouth is a rigid designator of the stuff that X is acquainted with that typically but not always has a good number of the following properties: it is potable, liquid, colorless, and odorless, falls from the sky, etc. For short, it is a rigid designator of the stuff X is acquainted with that is W. On this usage, "water" engenders centered content. It is a word for saying how things are with a part of the world, the part the user of the word is acquainted with (much as a petrol gauge is a structure for saying how things are with a part of a world, the part linked thus and so with the gauge). When X affirms "There is water somewhere," what she is saying is that the stuff she stands in the acquaintance relation to, and which is W, is somewhere. The way in which which centered world is the actual centered world determines truth at a world w is as follows: "There is water somewhere" is true at w just if the stuff which is W in the actual world, and is the actual center in the sense that it stands in the acquaintance relation with the producer of the sentence, that is, is the actual stuff the actual producer of the sentence is acquainted with, is in w somewhere.

This means that whether it is X or *Twin X* who produces "There is water somewhere" in the actual world can affect the truth of the sentence at w. From X's mouth, the sentence is true at w just if there is some H_2O in w. From *Twin X's* mouth, the sentence is true at w

just if there is some XYZ in *w*. For it is H_2O which is the stuff that is both W and stuff that X is acquainted with in the actual world, whereas it is XYZ which is the stuff that is both W and stuff that *Twin* X is acquainted with in the actual world. We can now give the set of centered worlds whose actuality is consistent with the truth of "There is water somewhere," on the meaning X gives to the sentence: it is the set of centered worlds whose center is the stuff that X is acquainted with which is W. For the sentence "Water is F" the answer is: the set of centered worlds whose center is the stuff that X is acquainted with which is W, and that stuff is F. And so it goes.

We can now give an account of how coming across the sentence "There is water somewhere" delivers information, which parallels the story we told for "I have a beard" in Lecture Two. We presume the account of "water" we have just sketched – henceforth, for ease of reference, I will sometimes call this use "standard"; it is the rigid use plus being *the* stuff which is W and is what the speaker is acquainted with – and that the account is known to those who come across the sentence.

1   You come across the sentence "Water is F."
2   You have reason to trust it.
3   Its ir-content is the set of centered worlds whose centers are stuff which is W, and that stuff is F.
4   In understanding the sentence you know in principle the set of centered worlds.
5   In understanding the sentence you know in principle how the center stands to the token sentence (it is that to which the producer of the token sentence is acquainted)
6   You know that you and the token sentence are in the same world.
7   You know how you are related to the token sentence and thereby your relationship to the center in question.
8   You infer that you yourself are in a world of the relevant kind, that is, its center is of the relevant kind, and how you stand with respect to that center.

The set of centered worlds is the ir-content of "Water is F." The informational value comes from (4) and (5) – your knowledge of the ir-content of the sentence *plus* your knowledge of how the center stands to the token sentence, provided the user of the sentence is using "water" as described above. The information you take away with you is recorded in (8).

Laying it out as we have can make things look more complicated than they in fact are. When you hear (see) "Water is F," you are given the information that the speaker (writer) is acquainted with stuff that is W and that stuff is F, by virtue of understanding the sentence. You know how you stand with respect to the speaker (writer) and thereby how you stand with respect to the stuff that is W that the speaker (writer) is acquainted with. Of course, given the caveats about our ignorance of precisely how one or another speaker or writer uses the word "water" – for the purposes of illustration we stipulated what X meant by "water," albeit with an eye to keeping reasonably close to what many mean – we have to allow that we don't know precisely what a typical speaker means by "Water is F" and so line (4) above is strictly speaking inoperative. But it doesn't matter. Near enough is good enough. We know the set of centered worlds that is the ir-content of "Water is F" in the mouths and from the pens of fellow English speakers to a degree that allows us to extract useful information.

11. The issue about narrow content[18]

Provided "water" is given the "standard" meaning, the worlds at which "Water is F" is true from X's mouth differ from the worlds at which "Water is F" is true from *Twin X*'s mouth, as we noted above. What is more, the sentences may well have different truth values. X's will be true just if the stuff X is acquainted with is F; *Twin X*'s will be true just if the stuff *Twin X* is acquainted with is F. As the stuff in question differs (it is H_2O for one, XYZ for the other), it may well be that one sentence is true when the other is false. However, the set of centered worlds whose actuality is consistent with the truth of "Water is F" is the same, regardless of whose mouth (or pen or keyboard) the sentence comes from. Ir-content is narrow. How can sentences with different truth values, different *actual* truth values,

---

[18]   The debate over narrow content calls for a book in its own right. What follows says enough, I trust, to indicate why I remain a supporter of narrow content despite the many attacks on it.

agree in ir-content? Doesn't intension determine extension?[19] But exactly this can happen when we have sentences with centered content.

Take the sentence "I have a beard." If Fred and I give the words the same meaning, then what we each say about ourselves is the same; we each ascribe being bearded to ourselves. If Fred is clean-shaven, then what he says is false, whereas what I say is true. Does this mean that the content of our utterances differs? In one sense of "content," yes – the worlds at which our sentences are true differ. All the same, the ir-content of our sentences is the same. How we represent things to be is captured by the set of centered worlds with bearded centers, and that is the set of centered worlds whose actuality is consistent with the truth of either sentence. This does not of course mean you get the same information (merely putative information in the case of Fred's utterance) from each sentence token. As we said in Lecture Two and say again just above, when we have sentences with centered content, informational value comes from putting together ir-content with the role of token sentences or words in locating the centers in question, and my sentence token differs from Fred's sentence token. It is like having two danger flags. They represent alike: *things are dangerous around me*, but they give different information by virtue of being different tokens of the same flag type.

What is more, we should want ir-content to be narrow. When we use space probes carrying instruments to investigate how things are in some region of space, we carry out a "before and after" exercise on the probes and their instruments. We survey the possible explanations of the changes in the instruments in terms of hypotheses about how things are in the region of space, and we take a hypothesis about Jupiter or Mars to be supported to the extent that it would provide, if true, a good explanation of the changes in the instruments. In carrying out this exercise, we take for granted the kind of difference principle we discussed in Lecture Three: changes that don't discriminate are of no use to us. If we are wondering whether or not there is water on Mars, an instrument reading that would be exactly the same whether or not there was water on Mars is of no use to us. We may have other reasons to favor the hypothesis that there is water on Mars, but the reading itself is no help. Or consider the

[19] See, e.g., Carnap (1947)

following passage from *Wikipedia* (as at March 1, 2009) explaining why doctors sometimes require us to have barium meals before being X-rayed:

> The gastrointestinal tract, like other soft-tissue structures, does not show clearly enough for diagnostic purposes on plain radiographs. Barium salts are radio-opaque: they show clearly on a radiograph. If barium is swallowed before radiographs are taken, the barium within the esophagus, stomach or duodenum shows the shape of the lumina of these organs.

This passage illustrates the fact that doctors take for granted as something too obvious to call for discussion, the principle that tests need to discriminate. The purpose of the barium meal is to ensure that different ways one's gastrointestinal tract might be correspond to differences in the X ray. Or, again, there would be something deeply confused about suggesting that a dye that turns from white to red if a tumor is malignant, and does exactly the same if the tumor is benign, is of any diagnostic value as far as malignancy is concerned.[20]

Now, as we noted in Lecture Three, there are a number of questions philosophers can properly raise about the difference principle. Why doesn't a dye's turning from white to red *as a result of the action of a malignant tumor* count as being different from the dye's turning from white to red *as a result of the action of a benign tumor*, in the relevant sense of difference? Or take the question as to whether the dinosaurs were warm-blooded or cold-blooded. What makes it hard is that it is obscure what difference their being one rather than the other would make to the fossil record. Why couldn't paleontologists short circuit the issue by arguing that a fossil record caused by the warm-blooded is *ipso facto* different from a fossil record caused by the cold-blooded? We know that there is something deeply misguided about this response, despite the fact, in effect noted in Lecture Three,

---

[20]   Although the dye's turning red isn't of any value in choosing *between* a tumor's being benign versus its being malignant, it can still be of diagnostic value more generally. Perhaps it is antecedently likely that one has no tumor at all, but if one does, it is very likely malignant. What is more, you know that the dye turns red if and only if one has a tumor. In that case the dye's turning red is bad news; it means you very likely have a malignant tumor. The change in color doesn't favor being malignant over being benign *per se*; it favors having a tumor over not having one, and one's skewed prior probabilities then do the rest.

§3, that it is no easy task to say exactly why. All the same, it is clear that there is some essentially correct insight behind the difference principle.

Now we can think of our bodies as kinds of space probes. We move through the world collecting information, or putative information, via the way the world affects our bodies and especially our brains. Our brains are important because they alone have the complexity and organization to encode and store a sufficiently wide range of impacts. Most of the information is at the sub-personal level but we know that some comes through to us at the personal level in terms of beliefs and perceptions, and here again the brain is especially important. We know that a good deal of the information is information properly speaking. If it wasn't, the tigers, deep ravines, and falling rocks would have killed us off long ago. We know that there will be an explanation of why we are good at collecting information properly speaking. The difference principle tells us that to the (substantial) extent that the beliefs and perceptions coming from the impact over time of the world on us are to be trusted, what we believe and perceive are a function of the distinctive effects of the environment, along with the nature of the bodies being affected. What matters are the impacts *plus* the nature of what they are impacting on.

This means we need a narrow notion of content for belief and perception; a notion of content, that is, on which what is believed and perceptually represented is a function of how one's body is, and the environment enters the picture inasmuch as it makes a distinctive difference to one's body, a difference that in turn feeds into personal level representational states like belief and perception, and thereby into the sentences we use to make public how we represent things to be. This narrow content will be the ir-content of our assertions.

Many will insist at this point that what I have just said cannot be correct. The ir-content of a sentence is a semantic property of the sentence, and we have a decisive argument that shows the semantic properties of sentences are broad. But which argument is the decisive one? Historically, the argument most often advanced is the Twin Earth thought experiment and we have seen that it fails. For example, in the remote part of the actual world version of Twin Earth, the only way to get the reference of "water" in the mouths of the

Earthians to differ from that of "water" in the mouths of the Twin Earthians is to suppose that "water" is used to say how things are vis-à-vis the user of the word, to include acquaintance in how we use the word. But that is precisely the usage that engenders centered content, and, as we saw, sameness of centered content is consistent with difference in reference and truth value.

However, many philosophers think of the broad content message as something obvious from the very nature of content. There was, they hold, never any real need for the Twin Earth thought experiment. Any content worth the name is truth conditional and semantic, and that's enough to show that it is broad. Putnam (1975) and Burge (1979) swayed us with their discussions of Twin Earth and like examples, but we could and should have drawn the anti-individualist moral without the aid of the thought experiments. Here is a statement of this way of thinking from Stalnaker:

> In retrospect, it seems that we should not have been surprised by the [anti-individualistic] conclusions of Putnam and Burge. Isn't it obvious that semantic, and intentional properties generally, are *relational* properties: properties defined in terms of relations between a speaker or agent and what he or she talks or thinks about. And isn't it obvious that relations depend, in all but degenerate cases, on more than the intrinsic properties of one of the things related. This, it seems, ... should follow from any account of representation that holds that we can talk and think ... about things and properties outside of ourselves. (1999c, pp. 169–70)

In some ways the tenor of these remarks is very much in line with the theme of these lectures. We should think of thought and talk in terms of representation and, especially, in terms of the way language represents that things are thus and so, by virtue of capturing how a subject represents things to be. This was how we introduced, in Lecture Two, the need for thinking of reference as a relation between language and the world, and the rationale for cashing this way of thinking out in terms of functions from words and sentences to possible worlds (or centered worlds when that is what is called for). This means that, *in one sense*, anti-individualism has to be true. To make sense of the representational properties of words and sentences, and of the mental states that are in the final analysis the source of those representational properties, we must think in terms of relations to the world. You cannot tell the semantic or psychological story solely in terms of how things are at and inside the skin. Here is a passage from Burge, making the point for psychological states:

> ... philosophy of psychology must do justice not only to the mechanistic elements in the science. It must also relate these to psychology's attempt to account for tasks that we succeed and fail at, *where these tasks are set by the environment* ... A theory that insists on describing the states of human beings *purely* in terms that abstract from their relations to any specific environment cannot hope to provide a completely satisfying explanation of our accomplishments. (1986, pp. 44–5)

We might put this by saying that a psychological states' *ecological job description* is essential to it.[21]

But none of this shows that content and intentionality, linguistic or psychological, is broad. Take Stalnaker's argument first. A substance's being water-soluble is a relational property in the sense relevant to the issue on the table. And it is a nontrivial example: a substance's being water-soluble is a joint effort between the way the substance is and the way water is. All the same, being water-soluble supervenes on the way the substance is. If a sample of sugar is water-soluble, then so is any chemically identical sample (as Stalnaker in effect notes, 1999c, p. 172).[22] We can make the same point using an example that steers clear of controversies about how to classify dispositional properties (some will dispute my classification of water-solubility as a relational property).[23] Consider a relation like being more untidy than holding between rooms occupied by teenagers. Its holding between R_1 and R_2 depends both on how R_1 is and on how R_2 is. It is a nontrivial case of a relation. All the same, if R_3 is a duplicate of R_2, then R_3 is more untidy than R_1 if and only if R_2 is more untidy than R_1 The fact that in nontrivial cases the nature of both relata (assuming it is two place relation we are talking about), come into play is perfectly consistent with the holding of the relation supervening on the nature of the relata.

---

[21] See Jackson and Pettit (1993).

[22] More precisely, any chemically identical sample in our world will be water-soluble. Change the laws of nature and you can change whether or not a given substance is water-soluble without changing its chemical nature. My defense of narrow content here is a defense of what is sometimes called the intra-world notion, as opposed to the inter-world notion. See, e.g., Jackson and Pettit (1993).

[23] Thanks here to discussion with Daniel Stoljar.

Burge's argument is equally by the way as far as the issue of whether or not content is broad goes. There are two quite different things that might be meant by anti-individualism about psychological states that can get conflated. One doctrine says that some given, central psychological property cannot be explained individualistically. This doctrine is certainly true, at least if we are thinking of those psychological properties that are representational, and it seems to me that Burge's remarks are entirely apposite if directed to this understanding of anti-individualism. The other thing that might be meant by anti-individualism is that some given central psychological property does not supervene on how the subject is from the skin in: it is, that is, not necessarily shared by doppelgangers; it isn't narrow. It is this doctrine that seems to me false for some psychological properties, and in particular for those that give a sentence its ir-content. Indeed, the falsity of the second doctrine flows from an appreciation of the force of the first doctrine, as we will now see.

One way to put this is by saying that a psychological state's ecological job description should encompass the totality of actual and possible interactions with other psychological states and environmental states. And that is a narrow property. The reason being water-soluble is narrow is that, for any two chemically identical substances, the totality of actual and possible interactions with water are identical. The same goes for ecological job descriptions. Duplicate me, and you duplicate how good or bad the two of us are at the various tasks that are, or might be, set by the environment. Another way to put the point is in terms of the value of information about possible as well as actual interactions with the environment. It is a commonplace that counterfactual information can cast crucial light on a person's psychology. Marilyn and Jane always go around together. Harry makes a point of talking to them whenever he sees them. Which one is he keen on? We would know if we had information about what he'd do in the counterfactual case where Marilyn and Jane aren't together.[24]

Why has the non-controversially correct version of anti-individualism so often morphed into the view that all content is broad? One reason is a misreading, as it seems to me, of Marr's (1982) representational theory of vision.

---

[24]   For more on all this from a perspective akin to ours in being against the current conventional wisdom, see Segal (2000).

Marr's interest is in how the eye is able to extract reliable information about the properties of what happens around us from their impact on the retina. This suggests to many that the notion of information he is working with is relative to the *actual* environment and is thereby broad.[25] However, Marr's focus in tackling the problem is, rightly in my view, on the *inference out* from what happens in the eye to the properties possessed by things around us. As he puts it:

> ... the true heart of visual perception is the inference *from* the structure of an image about the structure of the real world outside. The theory of vision is exactly the theory of how to do this, and its central concern is with the physical constraints and assumptions that make this inference possible. (1982, p. 68; my emphasis)

What is more, he is explicit about the material the eye has to work with: it is narrow. Here is how he puts the key point:

> First, suitable representations are obtained of the changes and structures in the image ... The result of this first stage is a representation called the *primal sketch*. Second, a number of processes operate on the primal sketch to derive a representation – still retinocentric – of the geometry of the visual surfaces. ...
> The important point about a retinocentric frame is that the spatial relations represented refer to *two-dimensional relations on the viewer's retina, not three-dimensional relations relative to the viewer in the world around him, nor two-dimensional relations on another viewer's retina, nor three-dimensional relations relative to an external reference point like the top of a mountain.* (Ibid., p. 42; last emphasis mine)

The task Marr set himself was to explain how, using as a premise *the way things are in the retina*, there could be a reliable inference to a property outside the eye. Below is how he expresses the problem for the detection of motion (I have italicized the parts where it is most clear that he is thinking in narrow terms):

> The study of visual motion is the study of how information about *only* the organization of the movement *in a image* can be used to make inferences about the structure and movement of the outside world. (Ibid., p. 159)

---

[25] Most influentially, Burge (1986).

But when is the inference out – the inference from things being thus and so in the eye to things being such and such outside the eye – reliable? It is reliable when it is almost certain that things being thus and so in the eye was caused by things being such and such outside the eye. In other words, what is crucial is that the eye be able to perform, so to speak, an argument to the best explanation.

Those who take the broad content moral from Marr's work often emphasize the (in itself correct) point that identical physical structures in different environments can carry different information about their environments. Internal happening I in structure S, located in environment E_1, may carry information about feature F_1, and when located in E_2 may carry information about feature F_2.[26] The point Marr saw so clearly is that in this case I is useless for distinguishing F_1-in-E_1 from F_2-in-E_2. This means that it is useless for distinguishing F_1 from F_2 in the absence of information distinguishing E_1 from E_2. If F_1 is a tiger and F_2 a pussycat, this matters. What we need are extant states inside us, and things happenings to those states, that are environment-independent, not in the sense that they aren't caused by the environment but in the sense that they carry reliable information *across* environments.[27]

It is time to talk about proper names.

12. Proper names and information (I)

I was cautious in my claims about how people use natural kind terms – or more precisely about how people use the word "water," but it is obvious that the points would apply to "aluminum," "acid," "gold," and so on. We surveyed possibilities; we didn't commit to one over the others. The situation with proper names seems to me to be different. I think we can be much more confident in our judgments about how people use proper names, based on what is pretty much

[26] "Internal" here means inside the skin. In the future there may be cases of 'assisted' belief via links between us and computers, of a kind that mean goings on in the computers need to be included. It is a nice question in the philosophy of mind how to specify the principles that govern where to draw the boundary.
[27] Of course the information often won't be carried by the environment's local impact but by the impact set in the context of a complex structure. The information supervenes on a big enough portion of that structure.

common knowledge about the linguistic practices of our fellow speakers and writers. True, if someone chooses to use "Julius" as a rigid designator or descriptive name of the inventor of the zip (following Evans 1996, p. 181) but keeps this a secret, or chooses to use "Gödel" for the person who proved the incompleteness of arithmetic but doesn't tell anyone, we won't know how they are representing things to be when they say "Julius was one smart guy" or "Gödel is famous." They will know but we won't. All the same, the situation for most of us with a great many of the proper names in general circulation, including the majority of those that figure in the philosophical literature, is very different from the situation with names of kinds. I think it is reasonable to insist that someone who does not know that proper names like "Plato," "Gödel," and "London," as used by most of us, are rigid designators is to that extent incompetent with proper names; they have a defective understanding of their role in our language. Fred can give his private meaning to "Gödel" but if he thinks his meaning is the norm or anything like the norm, he is wrong, and he is wrong in a way that shows he has not latched onto the role of proper names. Part of the job of a proper name in the language is to allow us to make counterfactual claims about the bearer of the name, and that is something we learn when we learn the language.

We use proper names to do what we noted in §4 above can be done by, e.g., "in fact." Newspapers, diaries, personal memoirs, works of history, writings in economics and social theory, and so on are full of speculations about how things would or might have been had Hitler died young, had Al Gore been elected President of the United States, if Sydney had been made the capital of Australia, etc. Often these speculations, be they well founded or not, involve throwing away in imagination much of what we believe to be true of Hitler, Gore, Sydney, and so on, including maybe the fact that they are named "Hitler," etc. In particular, we can suppose that anything and everything we use to identify, say, Hitler, in the actual world, everything that enables us to identify some person as Hitler, is not true of Hitler, and still have sensible discussions about how things would have been with Hitler, under such a supposition. What, in that kind of case, makes it the case that we are asking after Hitler and not Stalin or my uncle Jack, in the counterfactual world? There is only one possible answer: the person in the imagined counterfactual world counts as Hitler because he *is* Hitler, our Hitler. I am not saying that he counts as Hitler independently of his properties in the counterfactual world. I am saying that we can sensibly identify him as Hitler in our thought and talk about the counterfactual world, despite his having, in that world, none of the properties we use to identify him in our world. To make sense, as we manifestly can, of counterfactual speculations conducted using sentences like "Had Hitler been a weak orator, lacked a moustache, been called 'Jones' ... , then so and so," where the antecedent removes, so to speak, all the properties that we know belong to Hitler, we have to treat "Hitler" as rigid.

What about the role of proper names as conduits of information; the role we discussed in Lecture One and suggested was the picture that Kripke rightly saw as the core to understanding how we use proper names? For the reasons I gave in Lecture One, I think that this also is rightly tagged a folk view, one that is part of our shared understanding of proper names. The evidence I cited there, and I won't repeat it in detail here, is what the folk *do* with sentences containing proper names. What we do with them makes it clear that we – we, the folk – know perfectly well that tokens of "N is F" stand at the information-delivering end of an information-preserving causal chain, sustained by the way our language community uses the token name "N" that figures in the sentence, a chain which starts with some kind of baptism of the object the information is about. The token name ties the sentence to the object the sentence gives information about via the causal chain. I will cash this out in terms of ir-content and information value shortly.

Why are proper names so different from kind names in this respect? Why, in the case of proper names, is there less variation in usage between natural language speakers, and why are we entitled to believe that there is less variation in usage? The answer is that variation in the case of proper names would matter. We do not have a 'don't care' situation of the kind we have with "water." We know more than enough to identify water. If one person thinks that it is being the potable liquid that fills the rivers that's crucial, another thinks that it is being the kind that falls from the sky, whereas a third thinks that it is being whatever presents as a typically colorless liquid that is widespread, it does not matter much. The potable kind that fills the rivers *is* the kind that falls from the sky, and *is* what presents as a typically colorless liquid that is widespread. And we know that, and because we know it, we know there is no need to worry about the possible variations. The situation is completely different with people, cities, streets, and localized objects generally. There are an awful lot of them, and though they differ, one from another, in the absence of our taking special measures to make them different in known ways, they often fail to differ in ways we know about; they do not differ, that is, in ways that are of use to us in identifying them. And this matters a lot, as we noted in Lecture One. We want to end up in the place where the conference on two-dimensionalism is being held; we want our mail to end up in the right hands; we want to find our way around the streets of a city. We need, in consequence, to *create* or *make* distinguishing marks for the objects that matter to us, in the sense that it matters that we end up oriented appropriately with respect to them. And we need to do this in a way which is pretty much common knowledge. We don't want a system that helps the cognoscenti but leaves the folk in the lurch. This surely is exactly what we do with the whole box and dice of assigning names to things and agreeing, often implicitly, to use those names to convey information about what we have dubbed. Just as we said in Lecture One. And the system works, which tells us that the system is pretty much common knowledge; it is folk wisdom that we use names as elements in information conduits or channels, created by naming practices and usage conventions.

We can now spell out how names deliver information in terms of a shared ir-content for sentences containing a given name. The content is centered content, so an important part of the account will be our shared understanding of how token names serve to locate centers. The picture in the broad is like the one we gave for "I have a beard" in Lecture Two, with the complication that the link between token and center is more complex.

13. Proper names and information (II)

The ir-content of sentences of the form "N is F," for cases where "N" is used in the way rehearsed above and in Lecture One – the standard way, the way Kripke talks about – is a set of centered worlds. The reason is the same as the reason "I have a beard" has centered content. In both cases, we have sentences that give information about how things are vis-à-vis the token, which cannot be 'analyzed out' in descriptive terms. This is how "London is cold" in one mouth can carry information about London England, and, in another mouth, London Ontario. One sentence token is in the relevant causal relation to London England; the other sentence token is in the relevant causal relation to London Ontario. What we do when we produce a sentence of the form "N is F" is to participate in the process of conveying information about something that stands at the far end of an information-preserving causal chain sustained by uses of "N," that has our token sentence as the part of the chain which is located at the near end. Token sentences containing names like "London" and "Real Madrid" are non-natural versions of windsocks and the fossil record. A windsock carries information about the direction and force of the wind by virtue of its information-preserving causal links to the wind. The information is centered information, centered on the region of air movement whose properties are tracked by the particular windsock in question. In terms of centered worlds, its ir-content is a set of worlds with centers occupied by 'bits' of wind that have a force corresponding to how near to the horizontal the wind sock is, and a direction matching that of the wind sock. Similarly, fossils carry centered information by virtue of standing in, and being known to stand in, information-preserving causal chains that end in the fossils. The big difference with sentences containing names is that our observing a linguistic convention is essential to the sentences doing their informational-representational job. The needed causal connection only exists because of what our language community does, and the causal connection is known to exist only because we know what our language community does. By contrast, nature alone is enough for the windsock and the fossil to stand in the needed causal relations, and to know about the causal relations we need more than knowledge of how we use words.

In terms of ir-content and all that, here is how it looks.[28] The ir-content of a token of "N is F" is the set of centered worlds whose centers are F and were named (in the sense of being assigned a name) in such a way that the observance of the convention of using names in sentences to carry information means that the token of "N is ..." carries information about the center. The informational value of the

---

[28]   Thanks to Nicholas Shea for forcing needed changes to what follows.

token sentence comes from putting together knowledge of the ir-content with knowledge of how the token sentence locates the center and thus the object. The second bit of knowledge allows hearers to locate the center – the thing named – vis-à-vis themselves. Here is how it looks, spelt out much as we did for "I have a beard."

1   You come across a token of "N is F."
2   You have reason to trust it.
3   In understanding it, you know that its ir-content is a set of centered worlds whose centers are F and which were named in such a way that, in virtue of the observing of the convention of using names to transmit information, tokens containing "N" carry information about the centers.
4   You know that you and the token sentence are in the same world.
5   You know how you are related to the token sentence and thereby know your relationship to the center in question.
6   You infer that you yourself are in a world of the relevant kind, that is, its center is of the relevant kind, and you infer how you stand with respect to that center.

Let's note some properties of this account. They seem to me to be the 'right' properties, the ones we should want an account of the informational value of proper names to have.

First, one who uses "N is F" to make a claim about how things are, needs to know, or have justified belief about, just two things about the nature of N for their claim to be justified. First, that it is F, and, secondly, that it stands at the far end of the information-preserving causal chain we have been talking about, the chain whose near end is the person making the claim and the token they produce. In this way, the account has a 'direct reference' flavor. Reference is achieved despite a minimal commitment to the nature, in itself, of what is referred to. This is intuitively the right result. Take a well-worn example. I can use the sentence "Cicero is worth careful attention" to make a claim about how things are, and, let us suppose, a true one, without having any opinion about whether the Cicero in question is the Roman orator, the film, the spy, a dangerous dog in the neighborhood, the book, ... Maybe I heard someone utter the sentence. I was confident that they were observing the convention of using "Cicero" in a way that made their utterance a conduit of information. I joined the party in the sense of extending the information-bearing chain with my token sentence. That is enough to secure reference if there is in fact some object about which the sentence is carrying information in the requisite way. Of course things are different in the case of a sentence like "The *philosopher* Kant is F." In using that sentence to make a claim about how things are, one commits oneself to a third feature of the thing referred to, namely, that it is a philosopher, as is widely agreed.[29]

Second, in the simplest cases the name given to the object in the dubbing exercise that is the starting point of the information-bearing chain will be the same name type, more or less, at every point in the information-bearing chain. Most of us have the same name throughout our lives, although how much of the name gets used at any given point in the many information chains varies. I, like many, give my name in full in passing on information about my medical history but I leave out my middle name in passing on information about the authorship of an article. However, there are many cases where the name assigned at the beginning of the chain is somewhat, or sometimes very, different from the name or names later on in the chain. "Aristotle is a great philosopher," said today, gives information about the famous philosopher in virtue of an information-preserving causal chain running back to Aristotle, but Aristotle was not dubbed "Aristotle." The information-bearing chain starts with a dubbing[30] and, as the information is handed on about the thing dubbed, the token that carries the information at any given point transmutes over time in a way that ends with tokens of "Aristotle" in our mouths and from our pens and keyboards.

Third, often the information carried by sentences containing proper names is in part about the future. "The conference will be in London next year" carries information about how things will be. The same can be true of the fossil record. The fossil record may tell us that whenever global warming of the degree we are now experiencing happens, there is an extinction event 100 years later. That plus induction says something not very nice about the future. In the conference

---

[29]   For instance, by a direct reference theorist like Soames (2005b, p. 340), who calls such names partially descriptive.

[30]   A good question we won't be discussing is what it takes to be a dubbing, but see Kroon (2009) for some interesting discussion. Evans's Madagascar example, discussed in Lecture One, §3, tells us that initial dubbings can be trumped by later dubbings.

case, we get information about a future state of London by getting information about its past. The appearance of "London" in "The conference will be in London next year" carries information about a past state of London to the effect that, via decisions of conference organizers, it is the past state of something that has a conference-containing future state. And if it is the case that the information-preserving chain goes back to a past state of London Ontario, the sentence is about that London, not London England.

Fourth, because the reference of "N" is rigid – it refers to the *actual* thing dubbed in such a way that the token sentence containing "N" carries information about it, the way ir-content connects with truth is that the ir-content is the set of centered worlds whose *actuality* is consistent with the truth of the sentence.

Fifth, the account explains what is going on in the famous confusions over Paderewski. What happens is that the confused are right in thinking that, for each token of "Paderewski" in sentences they come across, there is someone standing in a certain relation to the token itself that the sentence carries information about; this is how they succeed in referring to Paderewski when they themselves use the name in observance of the information-transmitting convention. Their error is in thinking that the tokens of "Paderewski" that they come across divide into two classes: those that are part of an information-bearing chain that links them to a politician, and those that are part of an information-bearing chain that links them to someone different who is a pianist.

Sixth, the account is not a version of the description theory *if* by that theory is meant a theory that holds that "N is F" is equivalent to "The D is F," or to "The actual D is F," or anything at all like that. The ir-content of "N is F" is centered content; it is a set of centered worlds. Whereas the ir-content of "The D is F" is a set of worlds – the set where the unique D is F. Trying to find an account of "N is F" that is equivalent to "The D is F" by recourse to some fancy footwork with rigidity or with the description "D," is mistaken in principle in the same way that the corresponding attempt for "I have a beard" would be.

However, if you mean by the description theory a theory that affirms that a competent user of a proper name knows the property something has to have to be the thing referred to by the name, it is a version of the description theory. The role of proper names as information conduits rests on our knowing about the way dubbings found causally based information-preserving chains, as we have said a number of times. And, as we said in Lecture One, the idea that only philosophers know this is very implausible. It is common knowledge.

Seventh, we can now say a bit more about the objection from belief reports to the description theory of reference for proper names.[31] The sense in which the description theory is true, the second sense of the previous paragraph, is the same sense in which a description theory of "I" in "I have a beard" is true. Part of understanding the way "I" works in

(1)   I have a beard

is knowing that it refers to the producer of the sentence. What is the cash value of this? Sentence (1)'s ir-content is the set of centered worlds with bearded centers, and the token of "I" gives the information that the center is the producer of the token. And, as we noted in the first lecture, it would be a mistake to object to this account of the role of "I" that

(2)   My wife believes that I have a beard

is not equivalent to

(3)   My wife believes that the producer of "I have a beard" has a beard.

Why, exactly, would it be a mistake? Because the word "I" in (2) is doing its center-locating job. If I produce (2), I am telling you how to find the person *of* whom my wife believes he has a beard – look for the producer of the token of (2). I am giving you the 're' for her belief *de re*; I am not telling you what my wife's belief *de dicto* is.

Mutatis mutandis for proper names. It would be a mistake to think that the thesis that part of understanding the way proper names work is knowing how tokens of them carry information implies that

---

[31]   This is perhaps the most widely advanced objection to the description theory. The example to be discussed shortly is taken from Soames (2005a: see p. 421).

(4)   The ancient Babylonians believed that Venus was a star.

is equivalent to anything at all like

(5)   The ancient Babylonians believed that something named in such a way that the word "Venus" used according to so and so a convention carries information about it, is a star.

Why, exactly, would it be a mistake? Because the word "Venus" in (4) is doing its center-locating job. If I produce (4), I am telling you how to find the object *of* which the ancient Babylonians believed it is a star – look for the object the token name in *my* mouth carries information about. I am not telling you what the ancient Babylonians' belief *de dicto* was. Indeed I very likely do not know what their belief *de dicto* was.

14. Coda

These lectures had a circumscribed agenda. I wanted to outline a way of thinking about meaning that, while connecting with recent debates about the description theory of reference for names, two-dimensionalism, and externalism, was primarily concerned with making good sense of the way understanding sentences, and especially those containing names – proper names and names of kinds – can deliver so much information about the world we live in.

My conviction going into the lectures was that in order to make good sense of the connection between understanding, grasping meanings, and the acquisition of information, we need to: frame matters in terms of possible worlds; acknowledge that very many sentences and words have centered content; when dealing with sentences that have centered content, be clear about the distinct but complementary roles played by a grasp of ir-content and a grasp of the way linguistic tokens locate centers, in delivering information; and, finally, we need to appreciate the way rigidification induces two contents, one of which – the set of possibilities that might be actual consistent with a sentence's being true – is the key to correctly identifying ir-content in terms of truth.

That agenda has now been completed. We talked about a smallish range of sentences and mostly talked about rather simple sentences. That was in the interest of not obscuring the key points with too much detail. It will now be obvious what needs to be done: extend the basic approach to a much richer range of sentences in natural languages. That is a task for another time.

References

Ayer, A. J. 1962. *Language, Truth and Logic*. London: Victor Gollancz. (Original publication date 1963.)

Beebee, Helen and Dodd, Julian, eds. 2005. *Truthmakers: The Contemporary Debate*. Oxford: Oxford University Press.

Blackburn, Simon 1971. Moral realism. In J. Casey, ed., *Morality and Moral Reasoning*. London: Methuen, pp. 101–24.

Bloomfield, Paul 2001. *Moral Reality*. New York: Oxford University Press.

Braddon-Mitchell, David 2004. Masters of our meanings. *Philosophical Studies*, 118: 133–52.

Brandom, Robert B. 2008. *Between Saying and Doing: Towards an Analytic Pragmatism*. Oxford: Oxford University Press.

Brink, David 1989. *Moral Realism and the Foundations of Ethics*. Cambridge: Cambridge University Press.

Burge, Tyler 1979. Individualism and the mental. *Midwest Studies in Philosophy*, 4: 73–121.

Burge, Tyler 1986. Individualism and psychology. *Philosophical Review*, XCV: 3–46.

Burge, Tyler 1988. Individualism and self-knowledge. *Journal of Philosophy*, 85: 649–63.

Carnap, Rudolf 1947. *Meaning and Necessity*. Chicago: University of Chicago Press.

Chalmers, David 2002a. Consciousness and its place in nature. In David J. Chalmers, ed., *Philosophy of Mind: Classical and Contemporary Readings*. New York: Oxford University Press, pp. 247–72.

Chalmers, David 2002b. The components of content. In David J. Chalmers, ed., *Philosophy of Mind: Classical and Contemporary Readings*. New York: Oxford University Press, pp. 608–33.

Chalmers, David (draft). Frege's puzzle and the objects of credence.

Cullen, Simon 2010. Survey-driven romanticism. *The Review of Philosophy and Psychology*. Online January 30, 2010.

Davidson, Donald 1980. Freedom to act. Reprinted in *Essays on Actions and Events*. Oxford: Clarendon Press, pp. 63–82.

Davidson, Donald 2001. Epistemology and truth. Reprinted in *Subjective, Intersubjective, Objective*. Oxford: Clarendon Press, pp. 177–92.

Davies, Martin 2004. Reference, contingency, and the two-dimensional framework. *Philosophical Studies*, 118: 83–131.

Davies, Martin and Humberstone, I. L. 1980. Two notions of necessity. *Philosophical Studies*, 38: 1–30.

Devitt, Michael 1996. *Coming to Our Senses: A Naturalistic Program for Semantic Localism*. Cambridge: Cambridge University Press.

Devitt, Michael and Sterelny, Kim 1999. *Language and Reality*. Cambridge, MA: MIT Press, 2nd ed.

Devitt, Michael forthcoming. Experimental semantics, *Philosophy and Phenomenological Research*.

Evans, Gareth 1973. The causal theory of names. *Proceedings of the Aristotelian Society*, suppl. vol. 47: 187–208.

Evans, Gareth 1982. *The Varieties of Reference*. Oxford: Clarendon Press.

Evans, Gareth 1996. Reference and contingency. Reprinted in *Collected Papers*. Oxford: Oxford University Press, pp. 178–213.

Foster, John 2000. *The Nature of Perception*. Oxford: Oxford University Press.

Gettier, Edmund L. 1963. Is justified true belief knowledge? *Analysis*, 23: 121–3.

Goodman, Nelson 1947. The problem of counterfactual conditionals. *Journal of Philosophy* 44: 113–20.

Grice, H. P(aul) 1989a. Utterer's meaning and intentions. In *Studies in the Way of Words*. Cambridge MA: Harvard University Press, pp. 86–116.

Grice, H. P(aul) 1989b. Utterer's meaning, sentence-meaning, and word-meaning. In *Studies in the Way of Words*. Cambridge MA: Harvard University Press, pp. 117–37.

Jackson, Frank 1980. A note on physicalism and heat. *Australasian Journal of Philosophy*, 56: 26–34.

Jackson, Frank 1987. *Conditionals*. Oxford: Basil Blackwell.

Jackson, Frank 1992. Critical notice of Susan Hurley, *Natural Reasons*. *Australasian Journal of Philosophy*, 70: 475–87.

Jackson, Frank 1994. Armchair metaphysics. In Michaelis Michael and John O'Leary Hawthorne, eds., *Philosophy in Mind*. *Philosophical Studies Series*, vol. 60. Dordrecht: Kluwer, pp. 23–42.

Jackson, Frank 1998a. *From Metaphysics to Ethics*. Oxford: Clarendon Press.

Jackson, Frank 1998b. Reference and description revisited. *Philosophical Perspectives*, vol. 12: *Language, Mind, and Ontology*, ed. James E. Tomberlin. Cambridge, MA: Blackwell, pp. 201–18.

Jackson, Frank 2003. Narrow content and representationalism – or Twin Earth revisited. Patrick Romanell Lecture, *Proceedings of the American Philosophical Association*, 77: 55–71.

Jackson, Frank 2004. Why we need A-intensions. *Philosophical Studies*, 118: 257–77.

Jackson, Frank 2005. What are proper names for? In Johann C. Marek and Maria E. Reicher, eds., *Experience and Analysis*, Proc. 27th International Wittgenstein Symposium, 2004, Vienna: hpt-öbv, pp. 257–69.

Jackson, Frank 2006. Representation, truth, realism. *Monist*, 89: 50–62.

Jackson, Frank 2007a. A priori physicalism. In Brian P. McLaughlin and Jonathan Cohen, eds., *Contemporary Debates in Philosophy of Mind*. Oxford: Blackwell, pp. 185–99.

Jackson, Frank 2007b. On not forgetting the epistemology of names. *Grazer Philosophische Studien*, 74: 239–50.

Jackson, Frank 2009a. Replies to my critics. In Ian Ravenscroft, ed., *Minds, Ethics & Conditionals: Themes from the Philosophy of Frank Jackson*. New York: Oxford University Press, pp. 387–474.

Jackson, Frank 2009b. Thought experiments and possibilities. *Analysis*, 69: 100–9.

Jackson, Frank forthcoming a. Conceptual analysis for representationalists. In Julia Langkau, Christian Nimtz, and Hans-Johann Glock, eds., *New Perspectives on Concepts, Grazer Philosophisches Studien*.

Jackson, Frank forthcoming b. Possible worlds and the necessary a posteriori. In Bob Hale and Aviv Hoffman, eds., *Modal Content and Modal Knowledge: Essays on the Metaphysics and Epistemology of Modality*. Oxford: Oxford University Press, pp. 257–66.

Jackson, Frank forthcoming c. Possibilities for representation and credence: Two space-ism versus one space-ism. In Andy Egan and Brian Weatherson, eds., *Epistemic Modality*. Oxford: Oxford University Press.

Jackson, Frank and Pargetter, Robert 1985. Causal origin and evidence. *Theoria*, 51: 65–76.

Jackson, Frank and Pettit, Philip 1993. Some content is narrow. In John Heil and Alfred Mele, eds., *Mental Causation*. Oxford: Clarendon Press, pp. 259–82.

Kripke, Saul 1980. *Naming and Necessity*, Oxford: Blackwell.

Kroon, Frederick 1987. Causal descriptivism. *Australasian Journal of Philosophy*, 65: 1–17.

Kroon, Frederick 2009. Names, plans, and descriptions. In David Braddon-Mitchell and Robert Nola, eds., *Conceptual Analysis and Philosophical Naturalism*. Cambridge, MA: MIT Press, pp. 139–58.

Lalor, Brendan 1997. Rethinking Kaplan's "Afterthoughts" about 'That': An exorcism of semantical demons. *Erkenntnis*, 47: 67–87.

Lewis, David 1968. Counterpart theory and quantified modal logic. *Journal of Philosophy*, 65: 113–26.

Lewis, David 1979. Attitudes *de dicto* and *de se*. *Philosophical Review*, 88: 513–43.

Lewis, David 1981. What puzzling Pierre does not believe. *Australasian Journal of Philosophy*, 59: 283–9.

Lewis, David 1986. *On the Plurality of Worlds*. Oxford: Clarendon Press.

Lewis, David 1994. Reduction of mind. In Samuel Guttenplan, ed., *A Companion to the Philosophy of Mind*. Oxford: Blackwell, pp. 412–31.

Lewis, David 1999. Naming the colours. Reprinted in *Papers in Metaphysics and Epistemology*. Cambridge: Cambridge University Press, pp. 332–58.

Lycan, William G. 2009. Serious metaphysics: Frank Jackson's defense of conceptual analysis. In Ian Ravenscroft, ed., *Minds, Ethics and Conditionals: Themes from the Philosophy of Frank Jackson*. Oxford: Oxford University Press, pp. 64–84.

Machery, Edouard, Mallon, Ron, Nicholls, Shaun, and Stich, Stephen P. 2008. Semantics, cross-cultural style. In Joshua Knobe and Shaun Nichols, eds., *Experimental Philosophy*. Oxford: Oxford University Press, pp. 47–58.

Marr, David 1982. *Vision*. New York: W. H. Freeman.

Moore, G. E. 1929. *Principia Ethica*. Cambridge: Cambridge University Press. (Original publication date 1903.)

Perry, John 1979. The problem of the essential indexical. *Nous*, 13: 3–21.

Perry, John 2001. *Knowledge, Possibility, and Consciousness*. Cambridge, MA: MIT Press.

Putnam, Hilary 1975. The meaning of "meaning." Reprinted in *Mind, Language and Reality*. Cambridge: Cambridge University Press, pp. 215–71.

Ravenscroft, Ian, ed. 2009. *Minds, Ethics and Conditionals: Themes from the Philosophy of Frank Jackson*. Oxford: Oxford University Press.

Rumfitt, Ian 2005. Meaning and understanding. In Frank Jackson and Michael Smith, eds., *The Oxford Handbook of Contemporary Philosophy*. Oxford: Oxford University Press, pp. 427–53.

Segal, Gabriel 2000. *A Slim Book About Narrow Content*. Cambridge, MA: MIT Press.

Soames, Scott 2002. *Beyond Rigidity: The Unfinished Semantic Agenda of Naming and Necessity*. New York: Oxford University Press.

Soames, Scott 2005a. Reference and description. In Frank Jackson and Michael Smith, eds., *The Oxford Handbook of Contemporary Philosophy*. Oxford: Oxford University Press, pp. 397–426

Soames, Scott 2005b. *Reference and Description: The Case against Two-Dimensionalism*. Princeton: Princeton University Press.

Soames, Scott 2007. The substance and significance of the dispute over two-dimensionalism: Reply to E. J. Lowe, Frank Jackson, and Josh Dever. *Philosophical Books*, 48: 34–49.

Stalnaker, Robert 1984. *Inquiry*. Cambridge, MA: MIT Press.

Stalnaker, Robert 1999a. Assertion. Reprinted in *Context and Content*. Oxford: Oxford University Press, pp. 78–95.

Stalnaker, Robert 1999b. Indexical belief. Reprinted in *Context and Content*. Oxford: Oxford University Press, pp. 130–49.

Stalnaker, Robert 1999c. On what's in the head. Reprinted in *Context and Content*. Oxford: Oxford University Press, pp. 169–93

Stalnaker, Robert 2003a. Conceptual truth and metaphysical necessity. Reprinted in *Ways a World Might Be*. Oxford: Clarendon Press, pp. 201–15.

Stalnaker, Robert 2003b. On Thomas Nagel's objective self. Reprinted in *Ways a World Might Be*. Oxford: Clarendon Press, pp. 253–75.

Stalnaker, Robert 2008. *Our Knowledge of the Internal World*. Oxford: Clarendon Press.

Stanley, Jason 1997. Rigidity and content. In Richard G. Heck and Michael A. E. Dummett, eds., *Language, Thought, and Logic: Essays in Honour of Michael Dummett*. Oxford: Oxford University Press.

Stanley, Jason 2007. *Language in Context*. Oxford: Oxford University Press.

Strawson, P. F. 1990. Review of H. P. Grice, *Studies in the Way of Words*. *Synthese*, 84: 153–61.

Tichý, Pavel 1983. Kripke on necessity a posteriori. *Philosophical Studies*, 43: 241–55.

Tye, Michael 2009. *Consciousness Revisited*. Cambridge, MA: MIT Press.

Williamson, Timothy 2007. *The Philosophy of Philosophy*. Oxford: Blackwell.

Wittgenstein, Ludwig 1922. *Tractatus Logico-Philosophicus*, trans. C. K. Ogden. London: Routledge & Kegan Paul.

Index